HEROES OF THE SOUTH ATLANTIC

SOLDIER B: SAS

HEROES OF THE SOUTH ATLANTIC

Shaun Clarke

First published in Great Britain 1993
22 Books, 2 Soho Square, London W1V 5DE

Copyright © 1993 by Shaun Clarke

The moral right of the author has been asserted

A CIP catalogue record for this book is available from the
British Library

ISBN 1 898125 01 5

10 9 8 7 6 5 4

Typeset by Hewer Text Composition Services, Edinburgh
Printed in Great Britain by Cox and Wyman Ltd, Reading

PRELUDE

Phil Ricketts was having another nightmare based on fact. He was reliving with dreadful clarity that moment the previous year when, in a shit-hole of a housing estate in Andersonstown, West Belfast, Lampton had made his mistake and copped it.

They had moved out at dawn for a carefully planned house assault after being informed by the 'green slime', the Intelligence Corps, that a couple of IRA men were being hidden in the estate and preparing to snipe at a British Army foot patrol. As Ricketts sat between his mates in the cramped rear of the armoured 'pig' taking them along the Falls Road, secure in his assault waistcoat, checking his Heckler & Koch MP5 and adjusting his gas mask, he glanced out the back and was reminded again of just how much he detested being in Northern Ireland. This wasn't a real war with an enemy to respect, but rather, a

1

dirty game of hide and seek, a demeaning police action, a bloody skirmish against faceless killers, mean-faced adolescents, hate-filled children and contemptuous housewives. Christ, Ricketts loathed it.

He was filled with this loathing as the pig took him through the mean streets of Belfast in dawn's grey light – past terraced houses with doors and windows bricked up, pubs barricaded with concrete blocks, even off-licences and other shops protected by coils of barbed wire – but he managed to swallow his bile when the pig neared the estate and Sergeant Lampton, Ricketts's best friend, started counting off the distance to the leap: 'Two hundred metres . . . one hundred . . . fifty metres . . . *Go! Go! Go!*'

The armoured vehicle screeched to a halt, its rear doors burst open, and the men leapt out one by one, carrying their weapons in the 'Belfast cradle', then raced across the debris-strewn lawns in front of the bleak rows of flats, still wreathed in the early-morning mist.

Such actions were so fast, they were over before you knew it. Ricketts raced ahead with Lampton, across the grass, into the block and along the litter-strewn walkway as someone shouted a warning – a child's voice, loud and high-pitched – and a door slammed shut just above. Up a spiral of steps, along a covered balcony, boots clattering on the concrete, making a hell of a racket, then Lampton was at the door in front of Ricketts, taking aim with the Remington 870 pump-action shotgun. The noise was ear-splitting, echoing under the walkway's low roof, as the wood around the Yale lock exploded and the door was kicked open. Lampton dropped to his knees, lowering the shotgun, taking aim with his 9 mm Browning handgun as Ricketts rushed into the room, his Heckler at the ready, bawling for the bastards to surrender even as he hurled in a stun grenade.

The grenade exploded, cracking the walls and ceiling, but when its flash had faded away an empty room was revealed. Cursing, Ricketts and the others explored the whole flat, tearing down the curtains, kicking over tables and chairs, ensuring that no one was hiding anywhere, then covering each other as they backed out again, swearing in frustration.

'Let's try the flats next door!' 'Gumboot' Gillis bawled, his voice distorted eerily by the gas mask. 'The fuckers on either side!'

But before they could do so other doors opened and housewives stepped out, still wearing their nightdresses, curlers in their hair, swearing just like the SAS men and bending over to drum metal bin lids on the brick walls and concrete floor of the walkway. The noise was deafening, growing louder every second, as more women emerged to do the same, followed by children. Their shrieked obscenities added dramatically to the bedlam until, as Ricketts knew would eventually happen, the first bottle was thrown.

'Whores!' Gumboot exclaimed when the bottle shattered near his feet. 'And mind those little cunts with 'em!'

'Damn!' Lampton said, glancing up and down the walkway, then over the concrete wall, the shotgun in one hand, the Browning in the other, but briefly forgetting all he had been taught and failing to watch his own back. 'Let's get the hell out of here.'

That was his first and last mistake.

A ragged, gaunt-faced adolescent had followed them up the stairs and now emerged from the stairwell with his pistol aimed right at Lampton. He fired three times, in rapid succession, and Lampton was thrown back, bouncing against the concrete wall, as the kid disappeared again. Lampton dropped both his weapons and quivered epileptically, blood bursting from his gas mask, and was falling as Ricketts raced to the stairs, bawling, 'Christ! Pick him up and let's go!' He chased after the assassin, bottles bursting around him, the drumming bin lids and shrieked obscenities resounding insanely in his head as he plunged into the dangerous darkness of the stairwell without thinking. Then . . .

Ricketts, as he often did these days, was groaning and punching at thin air as he awoke from his nightmare. He soon realized that in fact he had been woken up by a mate, SAS Corporal Paddy Clarke, who was excitedly jabbing his finger at the TV in the barracks, saying, 'Sit up, Ricketts!' Everyone called him by his surname, or 'Sarge'. 'Look! A bunch of Royal Marines have been forced to surrender in . . .'

Gumboot started his weekend leave with a quick fuck with some bint he'd picked up in King's Cross. As he sweated on her passive body, propping himself up on his outspread hands, he was thinking about how the break-up of his marriage had reduced him to this.

Of course, he knew what had caused it – the good old SAS. His wife, Linda, had been torn between fear of what could befall him and anger at his going away so often. What she had hated, Gumboot loved – both the danger and the travelling – so what happened had to happen eventually – and finally did. Linda turned to another man, shacked up with him, and when Gumboot returned from Belfast, where Lampton had bought it, his wife and kids were missing from his home in Barnstaple, Devon, though a note had been left on the kitchen table, kindly telling him why.

Linda had been having an affair with a local farmer, James Brody, and had decided to move in with him 'for the sake of the children'. She wanted a husband at home, Linda had written in her neat hand, preferably one not slated to be killed or, worse, crippled for life. Sorry, Gumboot, goodbye.

Bloody slag, Gumboot thought with satisfying vindictiveness, as he laboured on the whore stretched out below him. They're all the same, if you ask me. He knew that wasn't true, but it made him feel good saying it – just as it had made him feel good when, in a drunken stupor, he had gone to Brody's imposing farmhouse, called him to the door, beat the shit out of him while Linda howled in protest, and then returned for another bout in the local pub. He had drunk a lot after that, mooning about his empty home, and was delighted to be called back to the Regiment and posted to Belfast.

Most of the men hated Belfast, but Gumboot had found his salvation there. Even the banshee wails of contemptuous Falls Road hags had helped to distract him from his sorrows. He had loved being in bandit country, away from Devon and Linda's betrayal – loved it even after Lampton bought it with three shots to the head. Blood all over the fucking place. Lampton dragged out by his ankles, down the stairs of the housing estate as Ricketts, his best friend, released a howl of grief and rage, then raced on ahead to find the killer.

No such luck. That estate was a labyrinth. The kid with the gun was protected by the housewives and 'dickers' – the gangs of kids who monitored the movements of the security forces and passed on the word. Ricketts had been distraught. Lots of nightmares after that. But Gumboot, though angry at Lampton's death, still liked it in Belfast.

Fighting was better than sex or booze, though few would admit it. In fact, this whore was pretty good and Gumboot was almost there, which prompted him to think of other things and delay his climax.

Sex was fine, but not enough. He needed to be back with the Regiment. Even when not engaged in a specific operation, he preferred it at the SAS 'basha' in Hereford, cut off from the normal world. A basha is the place where an SAS man is based at any given time – whether it be his barracks or a makeshift shelter erected in action.

Gumboot lived for the SAS. Life with so-called 'normal' people was boring and offered no satisfaction. Gumboot liked his bit of action, the danger and excitement, the thunder of the guns and the reek of cordite, and so he constantly yearned to be overseas, risking life and limb.

Even right now, as he climaxed, Gumboot was yearning for that. He groaned, convulsed and then relaxed. The tart patted his spine in a friendly manner, then glanced at her watch.

'You've still got twenty minutes,' she informed him.

'I'm amazed,' Gumboot said.

Rolling off her, he lit a cigarette and thoughtfully blew a couple of smoke rings. Then, realizing that he had nothing more to say to the woman, he switched on the radio beside the bed.

'. . . islands,' a BBC newsreader was announcing grimly, 'were invaded earlier today by . . .'

'Fucking great,' Gumboot muttered.

Corporal 'Jock' McGregor and troopers 'Taff' Burgess and Andrew Winston were having their regular Friday-night piss-up in their favourite pub in Redhill, Hereford, not far from the 'Kremlin' – the Intelligence Section – and their barracks. Jock was short, lean and red-faced, Taff was of medium height, broad-chested and pale-faced, and Andrew, who towered over his two mates, was as black as pitch.

Well into his third pint, Jock was staring up at Andrew, thinking what a big bastard he was, and recalling that if anyone called him 'Andy' they were asking for trouble. Born in Brixton, to a white man from the area and a black mother from Barbados, Andrew felt at home in England, but even more so with the Regiment. After transferring to the SAS from the Royal Engineers, he had soon become renowned for his pride and fierce temper. He was also widely respected for the bravery and skill he had shown during the SAS strikes against rebel strongholds on Defa and Shershitti, in Oman, in the mid-1970s.

Taff was a big man too, though not as tall as Andrew, and his smile, when he wasn't annoyed, was as sweet as a child's. On the other hand, when he was riled, he'd take the whole room apart without thinking twice. A good trooper, though, always reliable in a tight spot, and like Andrew one with plenty of experience of the kind that mattered most. Not bad for a Welshman.

'Now me,' Jock was saying, although it was not what he was thinking, 'I say that while it's nice to have a wee break, a long break is misery. Men like us, we're not cut out for all this peace. What we need is some action.'

'Oman,' Andrew said, nodding vigorously, deep in thought. 'Damn it, man, I loved it there. That desert was livin' poetry, boys, and that's what I'm into.'

'He even writes it,' Taff said, wiping his lips with the back of his hand and grinning slyly. 'I think it's a lot of shite he writes, but it keeps him from mischief.'

Jock and Andrew laughed. It was true enough, after all. Inside Andrew's huge, badly scarred body a fine poet was struggling to get out. Even natural killers like Andrew, thought Jock, have their sensitive side.

'I just do it for fun,' Andrew explained. 'They're poems about the Regiment. Some day I'm gonna put them in a book and give the book to the Imperial War Museum. Then I'll die happy.'

Human nature, Jock thought, studying his friend's ebony face and huge body. There's a tender wee soul hidden somewhere in there. Though at times, like when you're on an op with him, you'd never believe it, so savage the bastard turns.

'I'll die happy,' Jock said, 'if they just find us something proper to do, instead of more pointless field exercises. I don't mind a "sickener" occasionally, but now we're just killing time.'

'Right,' Taff said, swigging his extra-strength beer, licking his ever-thirsty lips. 'They pull us out of bloody Belfast, leaving only ten behind, and now they don't know what to do except keep us busy with bullshit. That's the only point of those bloody exercises – it's just keepin' us busy.'

'Also keeping us fit,' Jock said, automatically stretching himself, recalling the endless repeats of Sickeners One and Two – the four-mile runs, cross-graining the Brecons – running from summit to summit across the Brecon Beacons – setting up primitive base camps on the same freezing hills, the horrors of the entrail ditch, lengthy swims in OGs – olive-green battle dress – weapons and explosives training, map-reading, language and initiative tests, parachute jumps, combat and survival, escape and evasion – in fact, endless repeats of everything they had endured during Initial Selection and its subsequent five months of murderous tests – all just because they had no war to fight and had to be kept on form.

Jock didn't mind doing it for a purpose, but he hated time-filling. He didn't have a wife and kids – nor did Taff or Andrew – so like them, he wanted to be somewhere else, putting his training to good use.

'It was because of Lampton,' Andrew said, gazing around the busy bar, taking in the country-squire types and thinking what sheltered lives they led, insulated from the real world by inherited status and wealth, removed from questions of black and white, the crude realities of blood and bone. 'If he hadn't dropped his guard and copped it, we'd all be there still.'

That quietened them all a moment. They didn't normally discuss the dead – those who had failed to 'beat the clock.' Andrew realized that he'd said the wrong thing and felt bad about it. Embarrassed, he gazed around the bar again, reflecting that some of those privileged-looking old codgers had possibly fought in the last war, or in Malaysia or Aden, and might even be connected to the Regiment, which could explain why they lived here. You never knew if someone was in or not, so you shouldn't pass judgement.

'Look,' Taff said, squinting up through clouds

12

of cigarette and cigar smoke at the TV angled over the busy bar. 'It's a special broadcast,' he said. 'Something about an invasion . . .'

'Is that *British* troops we're seeing with their hands up?' Jock interrupted, watching the grainy newsreel images on the box. 'Where the hell is that?'

'Something about Argentina,' Andrew replied. 'Not quite there, but nearby.'

'I love her,' Danny Porter said without the slightest trace of guile, 'and I want to marry her and protect her always. I'm here to ask your permission.'

Danny was holding Darlene's hand in the tiny living-room in the small house in Kingswinford, West Midlands, bravely facing her mother and father. Mrs Dankworth was a fading peroxide blonde with a wicked sense of humour and too great a love of men, including Danny. However, her husband, Vince, was further advanced in his state of not entirely natural decay, with unshaven jowls and a beer belly, a face scarred slightly by a broken bottle in a pub fight. He also had a tendency to feel superior to most folk.

Vince Dankworth's sneer was presently reserved for the way in which Danny shamelessly held

Darlene's hand and kept smiling encouragingly at her, which hardly squared with the little berk's timid nature. He thought that Danny was a little berk because, although he was in the Army, he rarely talked about it and invariably mumbled evasively when he did. Vince was an ageing rocker and constant fan of Gene Vincent, after whose wife, Darlene, the subject of one of Vincent's great rock-'n'-roll laments, Vince had emotionally named his own daughter. In fact, Vince had originally been called Victor, which just about says it all.

Yeah, Gene Vincent! Now there was a real rocker. A gaunt, acned face, black leather pants and jacket, his leg in a brace which he pounded against the floor as he sneered and leered at the audience, before hitting the road again and smashing up some more motel rooms. The first really rebellious rocker, a bona fide original – not like that preening pretender Elvis Presley with his big, dark, girlish eyelashes and smarmy love songs.

Yes, Vince admired wild men – the 'bona fides', as he called them – and so could hardly accept that young Danny, who seemed so shy, even slightly effeminate, could actually be in the Army, let alone in the so-called Special Air Service.

Special for what?

Danny was 22, though he looked about 18. For this very reason, when Vince asked him what he had done in the Army in Northern Ireland and Danny merely shrugged shyly, mumbling something about 'not much', Vince completely believed him.

He would never have believed, on the other hand, that the shy young man sitting modestly in front of him had the instincts of a born killer and was renowned in the SAS for the number of times he had fearlessly practised the 'double tap' against known terrorists in Belfast. This involved entering incognito some of the most dangerous areas of the city to discharge thirteen rounds from his Browning high-power handgun in under three seconds, at close range, into his victim's body, then making his escape in a car parked nearby before witnesses had time to gather their wits.

Danny's ruthlessness was breathtaking, even to more seasoned members of the Regiment, but since such assassinations could not be sanctioned by the authorities, let alone recognized, he never received commendations and certainly never discussed his work with the Regiment. He would only say he was in the 'Army', mumbling uncomfortably when he did so, thus encouraging the former Ted and fan of greasy Gene Vincent to suspect that his daughter's baby-faced boyfriend was some kind of poofter.

Now the baby-faced, whispering poofter was asking Vince for his daughter's hand in marriage. Well, what could you say?

'Right,' Vince said magnanimously. 'I guess that's it, then. You want to marry Darlene – OK then, I won't stand in yer way. Me and Darlene's mum, we married young as well, so I guess we can't say no.'

He smirked at Darlene's bottle-blonde mum as she pursed her lips in a sensual 'O', blowing a couple of smoke rings, her bosom rising and falling impressively under a tight, low-cut blouse.

'Dead right,' she replied.

'Thank you, Mr and Mrs Dankworth,' Danny said. 'I won't let Darlene down. God, I'm so pleased. Thank you.'

'Yeah, yeah,' good old Vince said impatiently. 'Hey, love, you'll soon have a son-in-law. That should turn you grey!'

It wasn't the kind of house where you uncorked champagne, so Danny took Darlene out for a beer and a game of pool in the local pool hall, a right den of iniquity, to which he had been introduced by Vince.

'Paul Newman and Jackie Gleason,' Vince had said. 'That movie, *The Hustler*. A fucking master-piece, kid. A work of art. A real man's game, is pool.'

Danny, though not yet a man in Vince's eyes, had learnt the game quickly, but was careful never to beat his girlfriend's dad. With his dreamy baby face hiding the instincts of a killer, Danny knew exactly what he wanted – and what he wanted was Darlene.

'You probably think I'm pretty coarse playing pool,' Darlene said as they walked along slummy streets to the pool hall. 'But a lot of me workmates play it as well. It's the real gear around here.'

Darlene was a switchboard operator for British Telecom, and her workmates, as Danny had noticed, could be a bit on the free side. Danny, who had his innocent side, thought this was real neat.

'It's a good game,' he told Darlene reassuringly. 'It sharpens the reflexes.'

'Oh, you don't need *those* sharpened,' Darlene said with a surprisingly coarse chuckle. 'Your reflexes are *wonderful*!'

Danny blushed brightly with embarrassment and pride, which made Darlene love him all the more.

'God,' she said, 'you're so *sweet*.'

Which made him blush all the more.

Once in the pool hall, they ordered a pint of beer each and while waiting for a vacant table discussed when they should marry. As Danny was between ops with his Regiment, and therefore based in the camp in Hereford rather than in Belfast, they agreed that they should do it as soon as possible.

'I can't wait any longer,' Darlene said. 'Oh, I do love you, Danny.'

When Danny studied Darlene's sweet, moon-shaped face, bright-green eyes and jet-black hair, a lump always came to his throat. Now, with Willy Nelson singing 'Always On My Mind' coming from the radio perched high on one wall, that lump returned to his throat and filled him up with emotion.

'I love you, too,' he said.

He wasn't a man of many words, but Darlene didn't mind. She responded to his tender, loving nature and was touched by his reticence.

'That table's free,' Danny told her.

Though only five feet two, Darlene had a perfect body and long legs. She liked to show off in tight sweaters and jeans – to 'wind 'em up', as her mother had always taught her. When playing pool, which involved certain contortions, Darlene was a sight to behold.

Perhaps for this reason, a player at the next table, another member of the great unwashed – a ring through his nose, with another dangling from one ear, hairy chest bared in a leather waistcoat above black leather pants and tatty high-heeled boots decorated with skull and crossbones – eventually put his head back, blew a stream of cigarette smoke, and sneered to his mates, 'With tits like *that* bouncing on the velvet, how can she lose, guys?'

The sudden silence that followed was like an explosion, freezing everyone momentarily, as Danny spun his pool cue over, slid his grip to the narrow tip and brought the handle down like a club on the sneering git's skull.

As the lout howled and grabbed his head, pouring blood, looking dazed, Danny moved in without thinking to karate-chop him twice in the guts. The guy jack-knifed dramatically, making a strangling sound, and was vomiting even as Danny jumped back and again used his hand like a guillotine. This one chopped smartly at his exposed nape, for he was leaning forward, and he was face down on the floor in his own puke before he knew what was happening.

Danny knew he was doing wrong – using his skills for personal reasons – but his killer instincts were overwhelming, so great was his rage. He raised his right boot, about to break the bastard's neck, but Darlene cried out 'No!' and pulled him away, leaving his victim free to continue spewing on the floorboards.

'Shit, man!' someone whispered in fearful admiration. Then Stevie Wonder, who was singing 'That Girl', was cut off in mid-sentence.

'This is a special announcement,' the radio announcer said. 'Today, 2 April, 1982, a garrison of British Royal Marines guarding Port Stanley, capital of the Falkland Islands, was forced to surrender to . . .'

'The Falkland Islands?' Danny broke in, instantly distracted, no longer angry, and oblivious to the groaning man on the floor. 'Where's the Falkland Islands, Darlene?'

It was just another day for Major Richard Parkinson. As usual, he awoke at six in the morning and slipped quietly out of bed, letting his wife, Jane, get a little more sleep. Leaving the bedroom, Parkinson took the stairs up to his large converted loft, where he stripped off his pyjamas, put on a pair of shorts and proceeded to do 75 press-ups.

Though proud that at forty-four he could still do that many, Parkinson didn't stop there. Rising from the floor, his whipcord body slick with sweat, and then standing on tiptoe to grab the chin-up bar he had inserted between two cross-beams, he began his usual fifty pull-ups.

Most men half his age could not have managed this with such ease, but Parkinson, though a little out of breath, was otherwise still in fine shape when he finished. After a few more exercises – touching his toes and lifting weights – he went downstairs, into the bathroom, stripped off his shorts and stepped into the shower, where he switched the water from hot to icy cold. Cleansed and invigorated, he dressed in his freshly pressed OGs, complete with medals and winged-dagger badge, then sauntered into the country-style kitchen, located at the back of the house overlooking a well-kept lawn and garden and offering a panoramic view of the countryside. From here you could see the rooftops of Hereford and the spire of the church.

When not overseas or at the Duke of York's Barracks, in London's King's Road, Parkinson treated his wife to tea in bed every morning. He did this now, waking her up gently, running the fingers of his free hand through her hair as he set the cup and saucer on the cabinet beside the bed. Jane glanced up, smiling sleepily, then rolled away from him. The daughter of Lieutenant-Colonel Michael Lovelock – formerly of the Durham Light Infantry, then the SAS, a much-decorated veteran of Malaya and Oman, now in command of the Counter Revolutionary Warfare (CRW) Wing responsible for Northern Ireland – she was used to the demands of the Regiment and accepted her husband's unwavering routine as perfectly normal.

Parkinson returned the smile, but to the back of his wife's head, knowing that she would snatch a few more minutes of sleep, yet instinctively wake up before the tea was cold. After gently squeezing her shoulder, which made her purr like a cat, he turned and left the bedroom, automatically glancing into the other two bedrooms, where his children, now both married, had once slept and played. Reminded of his age, but certainly not feeling it, he returned to the kitchen to have breakfast and a quick scan of *The Times*.

His breakfast was frugal: orange juice, one boiled egg with brown toast, then a cup of black coffee. Parkinson did not believe in overeating; nor did he smoke or drink.

Opening his newspaper, he read that yesterday Argentina had invaded the Falkland Islands, overwhelming the single company of Royal Marines guarding the capital, Port Stanley. An emergency session of Parliament had been called – the first Saturday sitting since the Suez crisis – and the Prime Minister, Margaret Thatcher, was scheduled to make a statement detailing Britain's response to the invasion.

Parkinson immediately picked up the telephone and called his Commanding Officer, Lieutenant-Colonel Michael Pryce-Jones, at Stirling Lines, the home and heart of the SAS.

'I've just read the morning paper,' he said. 'It sounds serious, boss.'

'Quite serious, old chap,' Pryce-Jones replied, making no attempt to hide his delight at the prospect of war. 'In fact, *damned* serious. A bunch of bloody Argies trying to steal a British territory and we're supposed to sit back and take it? Not likely, I say!'

'Mrs Thatcher won't let them,' Parkinson replied. 'We all know what she's like. She'll insist that it's her duty to defend and preserve British sovereignty, no matter how small the territory involved. I think we're in for some action.'

'Damned right, we are. A task force of 40 warships, including the aircraft-carriers *Invincible* and *Hermes*, with 1000 commandos, is already being assembled, though the fleet hasn't yet been given orders to sail. The usual political posturing will have to be endured first, thus wasting valuable time, but war with Argentina is inevitable. By tonight, the United Nations Security Council will almost certainly be compelled to demand a cessation of hostilities and an immediate withdrawal of the Argentinian invasion force. Then there'll be negotiations. But cheering crowds are already gathering outside the presidential palace in Buenos Aires to celebrate the recapture of the so-called Malvinas, so it's unlikely that General Galtieri – he's the head of the military junta – will voluntarily back down. War it will have to be – and we'll be part of it. You'd better get in here.'

Parkinson hurried out of the house, climbed into his car and drove off at high speed, heading for Stirling Lines.

1

'I don't think I have to tell you men why you've been called back to camp on three hours' notice,' Major Parkinson said to his men on Sunday morning, 4 April, 1982, as he stood beside Captain Michael 'Mike' Hailsham of the Mountain Troop and Captain Laurence E. Grenville of the Special Boat Squadron (SBS), in the briefing room of the 'Kremlin', the SAS intelligence section at Stirling Lines, in Redhill, Hereford. 'Suffice to say that since its forced surrender to the Argentinians in Port Stanley on Friday, the unfortunate company of Royal Marines has been further humiliated by being forced to lie face down on the ground to be photographed for propaganda purposes. That's why you've all been called back. We can't let the bloody Argies get away with that, let alone their damned invasion of the Falkland Islands.'

'So why are we still sitting here?' Sergeant Ricketts asked.

'Right, boss,' Corporal Jock McGregor added. 'Our arses are freezing on these chairs while the Navy goes gung-ho.'

'True,' Major Parkinson said calmly, immune to their expected sarcasm, since the SAS not only used the informal 'boss' instead of 'sir', but also encouraged free thinking and initiative. 'A Royal Navy Task Force is set to sail from Portsmouth for the Falklands tomorrow. That task force will include frigates, destroyers, troop carriers, landing ships and supply vessels. Its two aircraft-carriers, HMS *Invincible* and HMS *Hermes*, will be crammed with Harrier jump-jets and helicopters, as well as with Royal Marines and Paratroops. Although she carries mainly Sea Harriers, HMS *Hermes* also has Sea King HC4s of 846 Naval Air Squadron, equipped to land the commandos with whom they normally train. At the same time, other ships will be leaving Plymouth to link up with yet more forces from Gibraltar. All in all, it will be Britain's greatest display of Naval strength since Suez.'

'But not including us,' Taff Burgess complained, grinning laconically at his fellow SAS troopers.

'Right,' Sergeant Ricketts snapped, not grinning at all. 'I've heard that the Royal Marines' special Boat Squadron have already asked for two divers – one a former Marine – to complete a team flying to Ascension Island, where they hope to join a British submarine in the South Atlantic.'

'*We've* heard, also,' SBS Captain Grenville said in his familiar terse way, 'that two members of G Squadron joined 2 SB Section at RAF Lyneham.'

'Yet there are still no movement orders for this Squadron,' Trooper Burgess said. 'What's going on, boss?'

Major Parkinson smiled. 'Oh, ye of little faith. In fact, earlier this morning our OC called the senior officer in command of the Falklands operation – Brigadier Julian Thompson, Commander of 3 Commando Brigade, Royal Marines . . .'

'Now on seventy-two hours' notice to sail for the South Atlantic,' Ricketts interjected sarcastically.

'. . . and insisted that he include us in the Task Force. He was informed by the brigadier that Naval and Royal Marine staffs are working around the clock to arrange the embarkation of the men and war stores needed to spearhead any reconquest of the islands. This operation has been code-named "Corporate" and we'll be part of it.'

'How?' Trooper Andrew Winston asked, rubbing his hand against his cheek and displaying an unwavering gaze that could make grown men tremble.

'Oh, dear, you trust us so little!' said the formerly renowned mountaineer and still dashingly handsome Captain Hailsham of the Mountain Troop.

Major Parkinson let the derisive laughter die away, then said in a graver tone: 'The Task Force has been gathered together to show the world, and particularly Argentina, that Britain is serious about the fate of the so-called Malvinas. It will therefore be leaving to military music and a lot of patriotic flag-waving, in full view of the assembled international media.' He paused for emphasis, before adding: 'But we'll be leaving as well. We will simply go quietly – flying out tomorrow.'

This time his men whistled and applauded, obviously pleased. Parkinson raised his hands to silence them. When they had calmed down, one of them, Trooper Danny 'Baby Face' Porter, put his hand up and asked: 'Do we have anything on the Falklands, boss?'

Major Parkinson nodded to Captain Hailsham, who said: 'Yesterday the Kremlin's staff gathered together all the information they could find about the islands in the MOD map-room – most of it from the British Antarctic Survey's HQ in Cambridge and other, more confidential sources. You'll find those reports in the folders on the desks in front of you. Make sure you know the details off by heart before we fly out.'

'Are there any contingency plans in SAS files or elsewhere for a recovery of the Falklands, if necessary?' the astute Ricketts asked.

'No,' Hailsham said bluntly. 'All of the long-term planners who considered it felt it would be next to impossible to sustain such a campaign.'

'How come?'

Hailsham nodded to Captain Grenville, who was in constant contact with SBS intelligence. 'The nearest feasible base from which to launch an amphibious assault is the very Ascension Island you've just mentioned,' Grenville said. 'That's nearly 7000 kilometres from the UK ports and airfields. As for Port Stanley itself, it's a further 6250 kilometres from Ascension – and there's only open ocean, apart from Ascension, between the UK and the Falklands.'

'That may be a problem for desk-bound planners,' Ricketts said. 'It's not a problem for us.'

'Correct,' Parkinson said briskly, proud to hear such a remark from one of his men and eager to jump back into the briefing. 'So tomorrow, 5 April, a small advance party from this squadron – the 80 men gathered together here – commanded by Major Cedric Delves, will fly out to Ascension Island to take part in the highly secret Task Force 317.9 – being formed to recapture South Georgia.'

A general murmur of approval spread around the briefing room, only silenced when Trooper Winston asked: 'Who divides and rules?'

'The work of all special forces, including the Special Air Service and the Special Boat Squadron, is to be coordinated through a command cell in Rear-Admiral Woodward's HMS *Hermes*, the flagship of the Royal Navy Task Force. I'll be aboard with some of you men.'

'Do you think there's going to be conflict, boss?'

'Not immediately,' Major Parkinson said. 'You'll fly out to Ascension and familiarize yourselves with local conditions as best you can.'

'What does that mean?'

'Ascension is a small island that can hardly sustain its civilian population of a thousand,' Captain Grenville explained. 'For this reason, the Royal Navy is going to severely limit the numbers of commandos and other forces who can be ashore at any one time. The opportunities for further training will therefore be limited.'

'Any more questions?' Major Parkinson asked when the silence stretched on too long.

'Yeah,' Trooper Gumboot Gillis said, licking his lips and grinning like a mischievous school-boy. 'Apart from its thousand head of human sheep, what else is on Ascension Island?'

'A British telecommunications centre, a US airbase, a US space-research centre, and a US gin-palace called the Volcano Club. That should see *you* right, Trooper. Any more questions?'

They all had a good laugh at that, but no hands went up.

'Then I suggest you all return to your bashas, open those reports, and ensure that you've memo-rized them by tomorrow. You'll be kitted out in the morning. Thank you, gentlemen.'

Major Parkinson and his two captains stepped away from the blackboard as the 80 soldiers pushed back their chairs and started to file out of the briefing room, most looking happy.

2

The selected members of D Squadron flew out of England on C-130 Hercules transport aircraft specially converted to flight-refuelling tankers. With their passenger and carrier holds containing long-range fuel tanks, the aircraft were short on breathing space, as well as noisy and bumpy, making for a long, uncomfortable flight that put no one in a good mood.

After landing on Ascension Island, the 80 men were driven in Bedfords from Wideawake airfield, located in featureless, wind-blown terrain, to be billeted in an equally desolate, disused school surrounded by flatlands of volcanic rock. There they made up their bashas, then attended the first of what would be many boring briefings from the 'green slime'. The Intelligence Corps staff informed them that no war had yet broken out and they would therefore be spending their days on the island undergoing limited, special training for the Falklands. This news was greeted with a universal groan of frustration.

'Christ, what a hell-hole,' Jock said that first evening as he drank beer with his mates in the Volcano Club, the American bar on Wideawake airfield, its windows giving a view of the rows of aircraft outside, including Vulcan bombers, Victor tankers, Starlifters, Nimrod recce planes and their own cumbersome Hercules transports. 'It's no more than a lump of scraggy rock in the middle of the bleedin' South Atlantic. What the hell are we doing here?'

'This is the nearest base for an amphibious assault on South Georgia,' big Andrew explained. '*That's* why we're here, mate.'

'And not alone either,' Taff said, sitting beside Baby Face Porter. 'Just look around you.'

He was referring to the other men in the packed, smoky bar, representing M Company, 42 Commando, Royal Marines, the RAF, the Royal Naval Aircraft Servicing Unit, Royal Engineers, and other members of the British Forces Support Unit. Though no more than a volcanic dust heap, nine miles across at its widest, the island had a BBC relay station, a 10,000-foot runway built by NASA, a satellite tracking station and a firing range. Now being used as a staging post for the Task Force, it was receiving an average of six Hercules flights a day, as well as a constant stream of men and equipment ferried in from the fleet anchored out at sea. As there was not enough accommodation for the personnel arriving daily, the men were forced to spend most of their time aboard ship, only being ferried to the island when it was their turn for weapons testing on the firing range, craft drills on the beach, other forms of training, or work. A lot of those men were here now, filling up the formerly quiet Volcano Club.

'Fuck 'em,' Gumboot said, polishing off the last of his inch-thick steak in garlic butter and washing it down with another mouthful of beer. 'Them Argie bastards made British RMs lie face down on the ground. I say crash a couple of Hercules into the fucking runway at Port Stanley. Two C-130s filled with our men. We'd have the Argies running like scared rabbits before we were out of the planes.'

'If you got that far,' Ricketts said. 'Rumour has it the airfield is ringed with 7000 Argentinian troops and an anti-aircraft battalion equipped with ground-to-air missiles. The C-130s, not fast at the best of times, would be sitting ducks.'

'Right,' baby-faced Danny put in, nodding emphatically. 'We would not beat the clock, my friend.'

'Well, when are we going to *do* something?'

'When the diplomats fail, as they will. Only then will we move.'

'Jesus Christ!' Gumboot exploded.

The special training began the next day and covered a wide variety of situations. Though the eighty-odd troops were already sweating in the tropical heat of Ascension Island, they were compelled to wear outfits suitable to the Arctic conditions of their eventual destination.

'The Falklands are notable for cold weather and wind,' Sergeant Ricketts explained as the men prepared. 'The two together can result in windchill, which can freeze exposed flesh in minutes. So you have to get used to operating in this gear, whether or not you like it.'

The 'gear' to which he referred was windproof and waterproof clothing which covered the whole body and was based on the so-called 'layer system', whereby layers of clothing are added or taken away depending on the temperature and level of activity. If moisture is trapped inside garments, sweat cools very quickly in the Arctic and the wearer starts freezing. Most of the

Arctic battle gear was therefore made from Gore-tex, which keeps heat in but allows moisture to escape.

Other items of kit distributed to the Regiment that first morning included mittens, face masks, ski boots, snow shoes and skis. Nevertheless, even kitted out like this, the kind of training the Regiment could do was fairly limited. Wearing their bulky Gore-tex weatherproof jackets, wool sweaters, Royal Marine camouflage trousers and heavy boots in the heat of Ascension Island was a distinctly uncomfortable way of undergoing so-called 'special training'. As for the training itself, given that the Arctic climate of the Falklands had to be simulated in a very different environment, very little new, relevant training could be managed. They tested their weapons on the firing range, rehearsed in canoes and Gemini inflatable assault boats in the shallow waters just off the beach, and practised abseiling from noisily hovering Wessex helicopters. But most of it was fairly basic stuff and all too familiar.

'We're just wanking here,' Gumboot said, summarizing the widespread feeling of frustration. 'Just passing time. Those Navy choppers are cross-decking troops every day, so they can be shipped on to the Falklands – it's just us being left here. I'm gonna go mad with fucking boredom if they don't move us on soon. Completely out of my mind.'

'Right on,' young Danny said, looking yearningly at all the ships anchored out at sea. 'I know what you mean.'

Pretty soon, just to keep the men busy, the instructors were resorting to the well-known torments of Continuation-and-Cross Training, including four-man patrol tactics, signalling, first aid, demolition, hand-to-hand combat and general combat survival. While most of it was of obvious use, it had all been done before, and after a few days the men were sick of it. To make matters worse, the Navy had placed many restrictions on what could be done on the island. This further displeased the members of the Regiment.

'I'll tell you one thing,' Corporal Paddy Clarke said two days later in the Volcano Club. 'I'm fucking tired of playing amateur soldiers every morning on this bit of volcanic rock – just learning the terrain and repeating the lessons of Sickener One. Then listening to the green slime givin' their boring lectures every bloody afternoon. Bullshit, bullshit and more bullshit. If we have to retrain, let's do it properly – not all this basic REMF stuff.'

REMFs was the SAS term for the boys at the back – the 'rear-echelon motherfuckers'.

'It's the Navy's fault,' Baby Face said. He was yearning for Darlene and looking lovelorn. 'As the Head Shed said at the briefing back in the Kremlin, the Navy's limiting the numbers of troops who can be ashore at any time – and that limits our training. It's always the Navy.'

'Right on,' Gumboot said. 'It's always the Navy's fault. They're just tryin' to take advantage. Those bastards want to keep us trapped here while they get all the glory.'

'No glory to be had,' big Taff Burgess pointed out mildly. 'At least, not so far. The politicians are still farting around while we sit here sweating.'

'Besides,' Ricketts added, 'it's not just the Navy. It's this damned terrain. We can't train you properly in this place because we've nothing to work with – no snow, no ice crevasses, no mud. Here we only have featureless terrain and sea, which is not much use to us.'

They all knew what he meant. The main key to survival in an Arctic environment is to get out of the wind and defeat the cold. For this reason, all SAS troopers routinely receive training in the construction of shelters such as snow holes, snow caves and igloos, as well as instruction in ski techniques and navigation in Arctic conditions. Special training in those areas was clearly impossible on Ascension Island, where the ground was too hard to simulate snow holes and too flat to construct dry ski runs.

'At least we've done some weapons training,' Ricketts said. 'Thanks for small mercies.'

In fact the only special weapons training they had done was in how to keep their weapons in working order in the dismal weather of the Falklands. Because in extremely cold conditions lubricants thicken, causing jams and sluggish action, all unnecessary lubricants had to be removed, with only the surfaces of the bolt being lubricated, and the rest left dry. Similarly, ammunition had to be cleaned of all oil and condensation. This required a little learning, but not much, so the men were soon bored again.

'Small mercies?' Jock said. '*What* fucking small mercies? I'm going mad doing nothing on this hell-hole while the task force sails on to the Falklands. I don't think it's right.'

'It's the Navy,' Gumboot said, returning to their favourite punchbag. 'Those bastards sail on to the Falklands while we jerk off back here.'

'I wouldn't mind,' Paddy said, 'if there was something to do here.' He lit a cigarette, puffing smoke. 'But there's nothing but this miserable bloody club and a lot of rocks and the sea. It's like being in prison.'

'Not quite, lads,' big Andrew said philosophically as he twisted a piece of paper into a tight ball and dropped it into his half-pint glass of Drambuie. 'Just take a look at this place. Here we are, in the South Atlantic Ocean, on what's essentially a piece of volcanic rock, only discovered on Ascension Day in 1501. There's poetry in this primitive place, man. Sheer visual poetry.'

'He's talkin' shite again,' Jock said, shaking his head in despair. 'He'll soon set it to music.'

A few of the lads laughed, but Andrew remained unfazed. He swirled the Drambuie in his glass, letting it thoroughly soak the crumpled piece of paper floating on top. 'Where's your sense of military history?' he challenged them, staring at each in turn. 'Did you know that this place was uninhabited until the British established a garrison when Napoleon was sent to St Helena in 1815? That makes a line of history from Napoleon to us, sitting right here. I think that's kind of magical.'

'Where's St Helena?' Jock asked. 'The other side of the island?'

'Seven hundred and fifty miles south-east of

here,' Andrew explained with a studied display of patience. 'A mere drop in the ocean. And to there – we're practically sitting in his ghostly lap – the great Napoleon was exiled. Now I think that's real magical, man – and magic is poetry.'

'I'm gonna puke,' Gumboot said.

'Don't blame you,' Jock agreed.

'I salute the great fellow-soldier,' Andrew said gravely. Then he flicked his lighter, set fire to the ball of paper in the Drambuie, put the flaming concoction to his lips and swallowed it.

It was the kind of sport the Regiment enjoyed and Andrew's mates all applauded. When he had finished his drink, the ball of paper was still on fire. He put his lips over the glass and appeared to suck up the flame. When he put the glass down, the fire was out. The men clapped and cheered again.

'Anyway,' Ricketts said when the noise had subsided, 'I think Parkinson should get on the blower and try to stir up some action.'

'Talk of the devil,' Paddy said, indicating the door with a nod of his head as Major Parkinson entered the bar and walked straight to their table.

'Evening, chaps,' he said. 'Sitting here moaning and groaning, are you?' The men jeered and howled melodramatically, until Parkinson pulled up a chair and sat down with them. 'Contrary to what you bullshit artists think, our CO has been keen to get this squadron embarked. He's therefore pleased to inform you, through me, that today he received a request for an SAS troop, the whole of D Squadron, to sail in the Royal Fleet Auxiliary *Fort Austin* for a proper assignment.'

Reprieved at last, the men roared their approval.

Some twelve hours later, in the grey light of dawn, the men of the SAS Squadron were driven away from Wideawake airfield, past planes, helicopters, fork-lifts, supply trucks, advance-communications equipment and stockpiles of fuel, rations and medical supplies, to the nearby beach, where Gemini inflatables were waiting to take them out to the fleet of battleships that would carry them on to the South Atlantic.

3

The 22,890-ton RFA *Fort Austin* sailed under the Blue Ensign in company with the large destroyer HMS *Antrim* (6200 tons), the frigate *Plymouth* (2800 tons), and the large fleet tanker *Tidespring* (27,400 tons). Maintaining radio silence, the fleet soon left Ascension Island far behind to become surrounded by the deep swells and ominous grey waves of the forbidding South Atlantic.

Although normally unarmed, the *Fort Austin* was carrying improvised weaponry, including GPMGs, general-purpose machine-guns. It had also embarked four Lynx helicopters specially fitted for firing the Sea Skua missile, and it was loaded with 3500 tons of ammunition, stores and spares. With a length of 183.8 metres, a beam of 24.1 metres and a draught of 14.9 metres, she was an impressive sight, and, to the uninitiated, overwhelming inside.

Spending most of their days and nights in the dimly lit, sweltering hold, in tightly packed tiers of bunk beds and hammocks, surrounded by dangling equipment and clothes hanging from stanchions, in a tangle of bags, packs, bergens and weapons, with little to do except be patient, the SAS men passed the time by studying as much detail of the islands as they had been given by Intelligence, playing cards, writing letters in which they could not state their whereabouts, visiting the latrines out of boredom as well as need, and exchanging the usual banter and bullshit.

'Here comes young Danny, just back from the head, getting his lovely Darlene out of his system by having a good wank. How did it go, kid?'

'None of your business, Gumboot.'

'Shot a healthy wad, did you? Enough to last you till tomorrow? Me, I can do it ten times a day and it's still not enough. That's why women can't get enough of me – because I just keep on coming.'

'They can't get enough of you,' big Andrew corrected him, 'because you pay them too much. The whores of London have never had it so good – at least not since your missus ran off and sent you on the prowl around King's Cross. At least Danny here doesn't have to pay for it. He has youth on his side.'

'Hey, look, he's blushing! Danny's face has gone all red. If he had as much heat in his dick, we'd all be in trouble.'

'Shut up, Jock,' Ricketts said. 'You've got a mouth like a sewer. Go and pick on someone your age – another geriatric.'

'I'm the same age as Danny. He just *looks* younger than me. That's because I'm a man of broad experience and it shows in my face.'

'Dissipation,' Andrew said. 'Your mug certainly shows that. Now me, I'm often mistaken for Muhammad Ali. Black is beautiful, friends.'

When feeling trapped or claustrophobic in the crowded, noisy hold, a man could make his escape by touring the immense ship and observing the constant activity that went on in its other holds and on the flight deck. Most of this revolved around the transfer of stores and equipment, either to smaller ships alongside or by jackstay rigs or helicopters to HM ships. The noise both above and below decks was therefore considerable nearly all day, and sometimes went on through the night.

'Fucking Navy,' Jock said. 'You'd have to be mad to join it. I mean, trapped on this floating factory for weeks on end with only the sea all around you. You'd have to be psycho.'

'That's what *they* say about *us*,' Andrew replied, 'and maybe they're right.'

'They're just a bunch of poofters,' Gumboot said, leaning against the railing and spitting over the side to baptize the sea. 'We've all known that for years. That's why they like life aboard ship, packed cosily together in their bunks. Why *else* would they do it?'

'Three days we've been at sea already,' Taff said, ignoring Jock's base observation and instead watching another helicopter taking off with a roar, silhouetted by a pale, cloud-streaked sun as it created a wind that whipped their faces and pummelled their bodies. 'One more day and I'll go mad.'

'Won't we all?' Ricketts murmured.

Luckily, they managed to survive the next day – and on the fifth, 9 April, *Antrim*'s fleet linked up with the ice patrol ship the *Endurance* 1600 kilometres north of South Georgia, and, escorted by it, began closing in on the island.

'Thank God!' Danny exclaimed softly, again leaning on the railing and gazing hopefully at the distant, as yet featureless grey horizon. 'Now let's see some dry land.'

However, as approval for the operation had not yet been received from London, another ten days passed before Major Parkinson could announce its commencement.

'How are the men holding up?' he asked Sergeant Ricketts.

'Not bad, boss, but they're obviously getting a bit frustrated. There isn't much to do down there in the hold except listen to the hammering of the engines, play cards, write letters, trade bullshit and take the piss out of passing sailors.'

'But no trouble so far?'

'Not so far – but their remarks to the sailors are becoming more saucy by the day, so there could be some punch-ups in the near future. There's a lot of energy needs squandering down there, one way or the other.'

'We'd better distract them.'

'I think so, boss.'

'Let's keep them extra busy, Sergeant. Every minute of every day. Otherwise, I'm afraid you'll be right and they'll start popping sailors. Let's burn up all that healthy, excess energy before they release it another way.'

'Good thinking, boss,' Ricketts said.

Within each of the four Sabre Squadrons of the SAS – A, B, C and D – there are four kinds of 16-man specialist groups: Mountain Troops for mountain and Arctic warfare; Boat Troops for amphibious warfare; Mobility Troops for operations in Land Rovers and fast-attack vehicles, as well as on motorcycles; and Air Troops for freefall parachute operations. However, during their training, the men must serve with every group, to make them adaptable to any of the four main forms of warfare.

Given the nature of the Falklands, the SAS men on *Fort Austin* were divided into the two groups needed for this particular operation: the Mountain Troop, led by Captain Hailsham and including Sergeant Ricketts, Corporal Clarke and troopers Porter and Winston, which would be used for land-based reconnaissance and engagements; and the Boat Troop, led by Captain Grenville and including Corporal McGregor and troopers Burgess and Gillis, to be used for any required amphibious landings.

The first group was therefore kept as busy as possible with interminable lessons on the geography and topography of the Falklands; the second with similar lessons on the tides and waterways of the islands and with the constant checking of their Gemini inflatables and Klepper canoes.

Nevertheless, life aboard ship became increasingly dull and frustrating, leading to restlessness, moans and groans and even an occasional angry confrontation between SAS Troopers and the crew. Sergeant Ricketts was therefore relieved when at last they were called to the briefing room by an obviously pleased Major Parkinson.

'I've just been informed,' he told his frustrated SAS Troop, 'that our accompanying tanker, *Tidespring*, is carrying M Company of 42 Commando, Royal Marines – destined to be landed in South Georgia.'

There were murmurs and many wide-eyed glances among the men.

'This island,' Parkinson continued when they had settled down again, 'lies 1300 kilometres east-south-east of the Falklands and, as the main base of the British Antarctic Survey, is particularly important to Great Britain. Its recapture will therefore be a clear indication to the world in general and Argentina in particular that if necessary we Brits will fight to recapture any territory stolen from us.'

'About time!' Gumboot exclaimed.

'Bloody right,' Jock said emphatically.

'Let's get them up and running,' Taff Burgess added, smiling at the ceiling. 'Let's kick the shite out of them.'

The ensuing laughter and applause were

silenced when Ricketts, on the ball as always, asked: 'Who's in charge *this* time?'

'The second-in-command of 42 Commando, Major Guy Sheridan RM, will be in command of the landing forces, including us' – a few groans at this – 'and he'll work with our CO aboard the *Antrim* in planning the assault on the island.' This brought more cheers. 'In addition to us, Sheridan has 120 men of M Company and about twenty-five swimmer-canoeists of 2 SBS, Royal Marines. There's also a small detachment of Marines aboard the *Antrim* with M Company's Recce Troop, a mortar section and the company OC. In all, about 235 men.'

'How many Argentinians are holding the island?' Ricketts asked.

'We don't know for sure. Why? Are you worried?'

'No, boss, I'm not.'

'I didn't think so,' Parkinson said with a grin. 'Anyway, we've just received a signal . . .'

'I thought we were sailing in radio silence,' big Taff butted in.

'It was dropped from a maritime reconnaissance aircraft,' Parkinson explained. 'A signal authorizing us to carry out covert recces on South Georgia.' This sparked off more cheering.

'As part of this, plans are being drawn up for our Mountain Troop to land north of Leith, where the Argentinians have reportedly been collecting scrap from an old whaling station. And 2 SBS will land about the same time in Hounds Bay, south-east of the island's main settlement of Grytviken, and move up the coast in inflatable boats to establish observation posts, which can observe the settlement from across five kilometres of open water. That's it. Any questions?'

'When do we leave?' Andrew asked.

'The operation has already commenced. On your feet, bullshit artists. We're busy at last.'

4

Because South Georgia was out of range of land-based aircraft, D squadron transhipped by Wessex helicopter from *Fort Austin* to the ice patrol ship HMS *Endurance*, which would sail closer to the shore, enabling them to fly in to their landing zone.

Looking down on the South Atlantic, where a man could freeze to death in a couple of hours, Ricketts wasn't the only one to give a slight, involuntary shudder, no matter how fearless he might normally have been. He was glad, therefore, when a streak of crimson appeared in the alluvial, snot-grey sea, then took shape as the hull of the *Endurance*, also known as the 'Red Plum'. Though smaller than the *Fort Austin*, the *Endurance* was equipped with two Wasp helicopters. To facilitate their landing, a large hangar had been built abaft the ship's funnel, extending her poop deck to create a helicopter landing pad. It was onto this that the helicopter containing the SAS team landed, bobbing up and down, to and fro, above the treacherous, surging, shadowy waves, before settling at last on the solid but constantly swaying deck.

Once aboard the new ship, Major Parkinson held another briefing, this one solely for the 16 members of his Mountain Troop, which would be led by the young and handsome, but decidedly efficient, Captain Mike Hailsham, and including Sergeant Ricketts, Corporal Jock McGregor, Trooper Danny Baby Face Porter, and the massive Trooper Andrew Winston.

Captain Hailsham was standing beside Parkinson throughout the briefing, which took place in a large, committee-room-sized cabin located above the flight decks, with drenched portholes giving a distorted view of the featureless grey sea and sky outside.

'Right,' Major Parkinson began. 'To put you in the picture, the Special Boat Squadron has been given the task of reconnoitring Grytviken and King Edward's Point while the Mountain Troop, meaning you lot, under the command of Captain Hailsham here, will be landed on Fortuna Glacier, South Georgia, to establish observation posts for the gathering of intelligence on the Argentinian forces. This may not be as easy at it sounds, for reasons which Captain Hailsham will now explain.'

Parkinson stepped aside as Hailsham picked up his pointer and tapped it against the map pinned to the board. 'The Fortuna Glacier is a potential death-trap,' he said bluntly. 'Its five arms flow down into the South Atlantic and are veined with hundreds of deep fissures and pressure ridges. At the top of the glacier, where the weight of the ice pressures downwards, it's comparatively level, but there are also hundreds of mile-deep crevasses. These can swallow a man up to his waist – though if he's lucky, the bulk of his bergen will break his fall and his colleagues will then be able to drag him out.'

This drew snorts of derision from some of the men. 'Don't laugh,' Captain Hailsham admonished them. 'I'm not joking about this. That glacier is massive, filled with crevasses, and extremely dangerous. In good weather conditions the procedure I've just described will be adequate to the situation, enabling us to advance, albeit slowly. However, in sub-zero temperatures and gale-force winds, which we're likely to encounter, it's extremely hazardous. In fact, sudden gales, which come from the mountains and are then funnelled down valleys, can produce gusts of over 240 kilometres per hour. To make matters worse, the weather's unpredictable. What may appear as a window of clear weather can be closed in minutes by whirling snow storms, producing a blinding white-out. So believe me, that glacier is treacherous.'

'Luckily, Captain Hailsham has Himalayan experience,' Major Parkinson interjected. 'That, at least, is a help.'

'If it's that hazardous, why choose the glacier for an OP?' Ricketts asked, thinking it was a poor site for an observation post.

'I have to confess,' Parkinson replied, 'that 42 Commando's second-in-command, Major Guy Sheridan, advised against it. However, the importance of that high point overlooking Grytviken and Leith Harbour, combined with Captain Hailsham's experience as a civilian mountaineer, was enough to make us take a chance and attempt a landing on this difficult LZ. We were encouraged further when we found that this ship carries detailed charts and maps of the area, now pinned up behind me.'

Captain Hailsham tapped the drawings on the board with his pointer. 'These plans of the buildings on King Edward's Point were carefully traced from drawings. The buildings housed the British Antarctic Survey settlement before the Royal Marines were forced to surrender to the Argentinians. The same buildings now house the Argentinian HQ. They're located at the mouth of a cove a thousand metres from Grytviken. That's what we hope to observe from the OP on the Fortuna Glacier.' After a short silence, Hailsham asked: 'Any questions?'

There were no questions, so Ricketts said: 'Silence is consent. I say let's go now, boss.'

'I always take note of the wishes of my men,' Major Parkinson replied with a grin. 'OK, Cap'n, get going.'

Captain Hailsham enthusiastically left the cabin, followed by the others.

The men prepared themselves with their usual thoroughness. Arctic cold-weather kit was drawn from the *Endurance*'s stores, including Swedish civilian mountaineering boots, which they used instead of their normal-issue boots. Weapons were signed for and carefully checked, including SLR semi-automatic rifles with 20-round steel magazines; 7.62mm general-purpose machine-guns; a couple of Armalites with single-shot, breech-loaded, pump-action grenade-launchers; M202s with 66mm, trigger-mechanism incendiary rockets; Browning 9mm high-power handguns; and fragmentation, white-phosphorus, CS-gas and smoke grenades. The weapons were thoroughly checked, then the machine-guns, rifles and pistols were cleansed of unnecessary lubricants, to prevent them from seizing up on the freezing glacier.

Other equipment, apart from food and drink, included a couple of PRC 319 HF/VHF radio systems and an older Clansman high-frequency set, which could also be used as a Morse or CW, continuous-wave, transmitter. Also loaded onto the troop-carrying Wessex helicopters were four sledges, or *pulks*, which could be hauled by hand and would be used to transport the weapons and other equipment from the LZ to the summit of the glacier.

When this vital work was done, the men gathered on the landing pads of the ship and took their places in the two Royal Marine Wessex Mark 5 helicopters flown in for this op from the fleet oiler, the *Tidespring*, and the smaller Wessex Mark 3, from the RFA *Antrim*, to be flown by Lieutenant-Commander Randolph Pedler RN. At midday the helicopters took off and headed for

South Georgia, flying above a sludge-coloured sea, through a sky ominous with black clouds.

'It looks as welcoming as hell down there,' Trooper Winston observed, glancing over his shoulder, through the window. 'It's just not as warm.'

'Getting cold feet, are you?'

'My feet are fine, Gumboot. I'm merely casting my poetic eye over the scene and making a measured observation. That landscape's as white as your face. Feeling ill, are you?'

'Very funny,' Gumboot said. 'The company poet has just spoken. He's trying to hide the fact that he's got cold feet by changing the subject. We all know just how white *he'd* be looking if he wasn't so black.'

'Now that's real poetic, Gumboot.'

'Thanks, Andrew, you're too kind. When you come down out of the trees and learn to spell you can write me up in your notebook.'

'Ho, ho,' Andrew said. 'A shaft of wit from the white-faced wonder. They grow his kind like turnips in Devon, where the folks all chew straws.'

'I like Devon,' Baby Face Danny, said. 'I once took Darlene there. We stayed in a hotel at Paignton and had a wonderful time.'

'In separate rooms,' Paddy said.

'Having simultaneous wet dreams,' Gumboot added.

'You shouldn't make fun of young love,' Taff Burges rebuked them. 'I think it's cruel to do that.'

'I don't mind,' Danny said. 'I know they're just pulling my leg.'

'To keep him from pulling his dick,' Gumboot said, 'which he seems to do all the time these days.'

'That's true love,' Andrew said.

'I'd call it lust, but what's the difference?'

'Now we know why your missus ran off,' Andrew said, flashing his perfect teeth at Gumboot. 'You were too sensitive and sentimental for her, too romantic to live with.'

'Now *that's* cruel,' Gumboot said. 'That's hitting a man below the belt. I could reply in kind by making comments about your girlfriends, but since I know that it's little boys you like, I'll keep my trap shut.'

'Little boys like *me*, Gumboot.'

'Yes, Andrew, I know they do. They like your nice smile, your black skin, your poetry and the fact that you have a dong so tiny you can slip it in smoothly. Say no more – I'm outraged.'

'Scared shitless more like it.' Paddy's grin was wicked. 'I can tell by the colour of his gills that he has constipation.'

'Scared? *Me* scared? Who said that? Stand up and be counted!'

'I would if I could but I can't because my poor knees are knocking. Yeah, Andrew, you're absolutely right: it looks like all hell down there.'

The bantering, Ricketts knew, was not a cover for fear, but a healthy way of psyching themselves up for the work to be done. Now, having exhausted conversation and nearing the LZ, they fell into a contemplative silence, each secretly preparing in his own way for what was to come.

Ricketts studied them with pride and a great deal of admiration. Trooper Danny Porter, who was a baby-faced Audie Murphy with the same lethal instincts, looked grave and almost delicate beside the enormous bulk of Trooper Andrew Winston, who was scribbling down his thoughts, or poetry, in a notebook, as he often did just before an action. Corporal Paddy Clarke, born and bred in Liverpool, was tapping his left foot and soundlessly whistling as he checked his SLR semi-automatic rifle. Trooper Taff Burgess, a beefy Welshman with a dark-eyed, slightly child-ish face, was glancing distractedly about him and offering his usual dreamy smile. Corporal Jock McGregor was rolling his own ciggies, which he would smoke at a later date, and displaying not the slightest sign of concern. And Trooper Gumboot Gillis, the small, sinewy, ferret-faced, former Devon farm-worker, was distractedly scratching at his balls.

All of them, in their different ways, were exceptional soldiers – truly the best of the best, a hand-picked elite. Which is why, as Sergeant Ricketts also knew, they were in the SAS.

Unclipping his safety belt, Ricketts made his way to the front of the helicopter, where Captain Hailsham was strapped in beside the Mark 3 pilot, Lieutenant-Commander Randolph Pedler RN. Looking out, past Hailsham's head, Ricketts saw a charcoal-coloured, snow-streaked stretch of mountainous land on a grey horizon, growing larger each second.

'Is that South Georgia?' he asked.

'It sure is,' Lieutenant-Commander Pedler said. 'And it doesn't look good out there. We're hoping to reach the LZ 500 metres above sea level, but I think we've got snow. That won't make it easy.'

Pedler was right. Within minutes the mountains of the approaching island could be seen more clearly and were covered with falling snow.

'You'd better go back and strap yourself in,' Captain Hailsham warned Ricketts. 'We're in for a bumpy ride.'

'Right, boss,' Ricketts replied, then returned to the main cabin to strap himself in with the other troops.

Nearing the LZ, they were met by wind-driven snow that created a 'white-out' by making earth and sky indistinguishable. Nevertheless, with the aid of the Mark 3's computerized navigational system, Lieutenant-Commander Pedler led the other two helicopters on through the dangerous gorges of South Georgia until the sheer face of the Fortuna Glacier emerged eerily from a curtain of falling snow. There they hovered, then ascended and descended, trying to find a place to land, with the roaring helicopters being buffeted dangerously by the fierce, howling wind.

The first attempt to land was unsuccessful, so eventually Pedler and the others flew away to circle the glacier in the hope of finding a clear area. They weren't able to land until the third attempt, later that afternoon, when the wind was blowing at 50mph. It was like landing in hell.

When the troops disembarked from the helicopters, or 'helos' as the Navy called them, the fierce wind was driving fine particles of ice before it. These stung the men's eyes if they were not wearing goggles and, more dangerously, choked the mechanisms of their weapons.

As they unloaded their equipment and long, lightweight *pulks*, they were sheltered from the worst of the weather. Also, the hot exhaust fumes of the helicopters gave them a deceptive feeling of warmth. But when they lifted off, the 16 SAS troopers, being suddenly, brutally hit by the full force of those biting, 50mph winds, realized just what they were up against.

'Shit!' Paddy exclaimed, wiping snow from his Arctic hood and examining the weapons he was putting onto his *pulk*. 'They're not only choked up – they're frozen solid as well. Completely fucking useless.'

'Damn!' Captain Hailsham exclaimed softly, also checking the frozen weapons. 'During the helicopter flight the warm metal must have attracted a thin film of water. Exposed to this damned wind, it froze.'

'Great!' Andrew said, rolling his eyes, then squinting into the howling gale. 'Weapons like ice lollies. Let's just hope the bloody Argies don't show up until we get them thawed out again.'

'The Argies won't show up here,' Ricketts said.

'Still,' Captain Hailsham warned him, 'we have to get off this glacier before nightfall. 'If we don't, we're likely to freeze to death.'

'Right, boss,' Ricketts said, forced to shout against the raging wind, but finding it difficult because his lips were already becoming numb. 'We better get going then. I suggest we break the men up into four groups, each roped together, and go down the glacier in arrow formation. That way, we won't lose each other and can help each other out if there's trouble.'

'Right, Sergeant, let's do it.'

After splitting up into four patrols, one of which included Ricketts, Andrew, Danny, and Paddy, the men attached themselves to the *pulks* loaded with food and ammunition, roped themselves together in four separate groups, then advanced down the glacier in arrowhead formation, inhuman in their bulky Arctic suits and hoods, ghostlike in the mist and swirling snow.

One patrol had orders to watch Leith, one Stromness and one Husvik, four miles from the LZ. The fourth, led by Ricketts, had intended going down the opposite west slope to recce Fortuna Bay for boat and helicopter landing points. However, this was not to be. As the men edged slowly forward, the storm actually grew worse, with the wind howling louder and the snow thickening around them, reducing visibility to almost zero.

The ice surface of the glacier was covered with snow, which was gathering in the crevasses. The men could not always see the indentations in the snow, and within a few metres they came to a halt when young Danny became the first to cry out instinctively as he plunged through the snow-covered ice.

His fall was stopped by his bergen, his backpack, straddling the fissure, leaving him buried from the waist down.

'Christ!' he cried, frantically waving his hands above his head. 'Get me outta here!'

'Don't move!' Ricketts called to him, tugging on the rope, meanwhile pulling himself forward to anchor Danny with his pickaxe and prevent him sinking deeper into the crevasse. Andrew and Paddy then did the same, hooking their pickaxes under Danny's armpits, then taking hold of his shoulders to pull him back up to solid ground.

Once Danny had shaken off the snow and ice, they all stepped over the crevasse, leaned into the wind and continued their advance down the white, gleaming side of the glacier. Then Paddy fell into another crevasse, compelling them to stop and start the rescue procedure all over again.

This occurred repeatedly, to one man after another. It was also happening to the other groups, whom Ricketts could see as shadowy, inhuman shapes in the snow storm, clearly struggling yet making little progress.

As the storm grew worse, their advance was reduced to a snail's pace. By nightfall, when already they were frozen and exhausted, they had managed to cover only about half a mile.

'I'm afraid Sheridan was right!' Captain Hailsham shouted to Ricketts. 'We're wasting our time here!'

Unable to do more in the relentless, continuing snow storm, the four patrols regrouped in the gathering gloom of the evening and attempted to make camp for the night. Seeking protection from the piercing cold, they found the least exposed part of the glacier, under a rock outcrop, and there tried to put up three-man tents. When these were whipped away by the violent gale, snapping like living things as they disappeared in the darkness, the men dug snow holes and attempted to sleep in 'bivvy bags' with their boots on. By midnight, however, hurricane force 11 winds were howling over the mountains, which not only prevented sleep, but also brought a real risk of hypothermia and frostbite. At this point, the experience of Captain Hailsham told him to give up.

'The troop will have to be withdrawn as soon as possible,' he informed Ricketts. 'Otherwise, the frostbite could become so acute that some of us might even lose our limbs. Get on that radio, Sergeant, and tell them to lift us out.'

Using the PRC 319 HF/VHF radio system, Ricketts did as he was told, and was soon in touch with HMS *Endurance*. He was informed that three Wessex helicopters would be despatched early the next morning, one from the *Antrim*, the other from HMS *Tidespring*, and that he was to send up a SARBE, or surface-to-air rescue beacon, when he saw them.

'We're freezing our balls off here,' Ricketts said, 'and it's getting worse every minute, so try getting to us as soon as possible. Over.'

'First light, on the nose,' he was informed. 'Over and out.'

'Fucking first light,' Paddy spluttered when informed that he would be spending the rest of the night on the glacier. 'They'll be too busy banging each other in their bunks to give us a thought. Typical fucking Navy! Just leave us to get hypothermia or frostbite, while they warm themselves by getting it up the rear end. I'm pissed off, I can tell you!'

'They can't fly in this storm in the dark,' Ricketts explained. 'It's as simple as that. Now get as deep down in those holes as you can go, lads. Don't let the cold get to you.'

'Right, boss,' Andrew replied. 'Think of your darling Darlene,' he then said to Danny, who was expertly digging in beside him. 'That should keep *you* warm, mate!'

'Aw, knock it off,' said Danny, embarrassed, before turning away and curling up in his bivvy bag. 'You're just trying to make me blush.'

'Some ladies like guys who blush,' Andrew replied, wriggling into his own bivvy bag as the snow fell on him. 'They'd drop their knickers at the very sight of a flushed male face.'

'You're so crude,' Danny complained.

'He wants you blushing,' Paddy said, ''cause when you do, we don't need the beacons. Your face glows in the dark.'

'OK,' Ricketts said when the laughter died down, 'that's enough of the bullshit. Now let's all get some shut-eye.'

'Yes, boss,' they replied.

The banter was a necessary antidote to the appalling conditions, for the ensuing night was hellish, with the hurricane force 11 wind not abating at all, and the snow and ice beating at them every second, instantly flaying them if they made the mistake of exposing a patch of skin to the elements. Sleep was impossible, or at least came in fits and starts, and by dawn, when a pale sun shone through, they were exhausted and numb.

The Navy pilots were as good as their word. Even before he heard them – since the wind was still roaring, the sweeping snow still hissing – Ricketts saw the three Wessex helicopters coming in to attempt a landing on the glacier and pick them up. Wriggling quickly out of his bivvy bag, he sent up a beacon as the rest of the group came back to life, smacking the snow off their hoods and gloves, then slapping themselves to get their circulation going.

'What a bloody disaster!' Paddy said. 'A complete waste of time!'

'Shut up, Trooper,' Ricketts barked at him while watching the green smoke of his chemical flare spreading through the still dark, cloudy and snow-streaked sky directly above.

Contacting the helo on the PRC 319, he learnt that the lead pilot in the Mark 3 was again

Lieutenant-Commander Pedler, who had brought them here, and that he had spotted them and was coming in for a landing. The Mark 3 duly descended through the raging blizzard, its rotors causing a more violent snowstorm as it nervously touched down. It was followed immediately by the other two helicopters.

'You're a sight for sore eyes,' Captain Hailsham shouted at Lieutenant-Commander Pedler.

'You can sing my praises later,' Pedler replied. 'For now, let's load up and take off. This damned storm's getting worse.'

As quickly as possible, given the appalling conditions, the men distributed their equipment to the three helicopters, then took their own places. Pedler's Mark 3 lifted off first, followed by the two Mark 5s, one of which was carrying Captain Hailsham, Ricketts, Paddy Clarke, young Danny and big Andrew.

'Good riddance,' the latter said, looking down on the gleaming, storm-swept glacier as the chopper ascended.

'The most useless bloody op I've ever been on,' Paddy said, wiping the melting snow from his face. 'A complete waste of time.'

'Shut it, troopers,' Ricketts admonished them, glancing through the window. 'No need for . . .'

70

He stopped in mid-sentence when he saw the other Mark 5 flying into a particularly fierce gust of snow, a virtual white-out, that appeared to be forcing it off course, then back down, nose first, to the ground. 'Oh, Christ!' Ricketts groaned as the Mark 5 wobbled widely, clearly fighting to right itself, then went down, crashing into the glacier in a mess of buckling skis, breaking rotors and flying glass, all of which was obscured in geysering snow.

The helicopter shuddered like a dying elephant as the snow fell on it.

'They went down!' Danny shouted involuntarily.

Even as the Mark 5 crashed, Ricketts heard Pedler's voice coming over the radio, saying that he was going to land again on a rescue mission.

'Message received,' the pilot up ahead said. 'We're coming down after you. Over and out.'

'Damned right, we are,' Andrew said.

Ricketts saw Pedler's Mark 3 turn back and descend, straight back into the blizzard, until it had practically disappeared in the swirling snow. The remaining Mark 5 followed suit, turning back to where they had come from, and soon it too was enveloped in a thick curtain of swirling snow.

It was virtually another white-out, with glacier

and sky indistinguishable, but then the snow thinned a little and Ricketts saw the Mark 3 landing, its spinning rotors sweeping up more snow and hurling it over the crashed aircraft, from which he could make out some figures emerging.

The wall of the glacier was now directly outside the window of the Mark 5, appearing to rise rapidly as the helicopter descended, then the rotors whipped up more snow as it settled down on its skis, bounced a little and stopped.

'Let's go!' Captain Hailsham called out.

Ricketts and his men all jumped out of the helicopter, intent on a rescue operation. But when they had disembarked and crossed to the Mark 3, positioned beside the crashed Mark 5, they found Pedler's men already helping the survivors into their own helo, all of them looking eerily unnatural in their bulky Arctic outfits, spectral in the blizzard.

An SAS corporal, a new man, was the only person injured of the seven aboard. Even though the pilot's cabin had been smashed to hell, the pilot was all right.

'Our helo can hold more men than yours,' Lieutenant-Commander Collins, the Royal Navy pilot of the Mark 5, reminded Lieutenant-Commander Pedler, 'so you take three, including the injured man, and we'll take the other four.'

'Right,' Pedler said. 'Thanks. Let's hope we get the hell out of here.'

'I recommend the ditching of everything but weapons and belt equipment. You could also lighten your helo by leaving some of its special equipment on the ground.'

'Good thinking. Let's do it. Fix it up, Cap'n.'

Hailsham called the men together to tell them what he wanted. When the men had done as they were told, discarding everything but weapons and belt equipment, and the Mark 3 had been stripped of some of its special equipment, which was hastily buried under the ice and snow, the men were distributed between the two operational helicopters and they took off again.

The Mark 5 had barely lifted off the ground when it flew into a white-out, was buffeted by a fierce wind and, with its heavy load, became the second to crash. Ricketts felt the helo shaking like a car with punctured tyres, then it tilted to one side, showing the ground directly below, and the pilot called out a warning just before it went down.

'Oh, Christ, not again!' young Danny cried out in disbelief.

'Hold on!' Ricketts bawled.

The rotor blades made contact first, snapping off and spinning away, then the skis buckled beneath the crashing fuselage, making the helo tilt further. The men inside were scattered like skittles, hurled against each other, and scrambled about on the floor of the passenger cabin, cursing loudly, as their weapons and other equipment were thrown about, clattering all around them.

The helo shuddered and shrieked, its metal buckling, glass breaking, then it quivered in the swirling snow and sank into impacted ice.

'Jesus Christ!' Andrew exploded, picking himself up and glancing at the mess all around him. 'I don't believe this shit, man.'

'All out!' Captain Hailsham bawled, as he and the pilot unbuckled their safety belts and turned back into the disordered passenger cabin.

'Not again!' Danny complained. 'I can't stand it out there.'

'Out!' Ricketts bawled. '*Out!*'

Amazingly, no one had been hurt and all of the men made their escape from the wreckage, dropping down onto the ice and snow, back into the raging storm and its fiercely swirling sleet.

Even before the last man had emerged, Pedler's helicopter became visible in the stormy sky as he courageously returned to the glacier, checking out their location.

'Is that radio working?' Captain Hailsham wanted to know.

'Yes, sir,' Ricketts said. 'I'm trying to get in touch with them right now. Zulu to Tiger, Zulu to Tiger. Can you hear me? Over.'

'Tiger to Zulu, Tiger to Zulu. I hear you loud and clear. We're short on fuel up here, so we can't land again. You'll have to hang in there until I get back to the *Antrim* and top up the tanks. What's the damage down there? Over.'

'Zulu to Tiger. Zulu to Tiger. The helo's a write-off, but no one's been hurt. We'll try to survive here as best we can, but you better be quick. It's below freezing here. Over.'

'Tiger to Zulu. Tiger to Zulu. I have your position and I'll be back. Over and out.'

Ricketts turned off his microphone as the helicopter high above turned away and headed back out to sea, soon disappearing beyond a broad bank of dense clouds and dark sky.

'I still don't believe this shit, man,' Andrew groaned. 'What a fucking disaster!'

'That Major Sheridan advised us against it,' Danny reminded them. 'He's probably smirking right now.'

'He won't be smirking, Trooper,' Ricketts said, 'so there's no need for that talk. What's done has been done, so let's just settle in here as best we can and wait for the helo. Let's not freeze to death here.'

'Sergeant Ricketts is right,' Captain Hailsham said. 'We run the risk of hypothermia or frost-bite, so let's take special care. Belt in and wrap up, men.'

This, Ricketts knew, would be the worst time for all of them – the time when the strongest man could break. First the failure of the mission, then a night of hellish cold, followed by two helicopter crashes in a row, now being trapped here again. The physical enemy was the cold, but the loss of morale could be more dangerous, particularly if it led to self-pity or a sense of despair.

However, this was exactly the kind of situation the SAS were trained for, both physically and psychologically, and Ricketts was pleased to see his 15 remaining men rising to the challenge by making themselves as comfort-able as they could, with only one survival tent and hardly any kit, even as the snow continued falling and gradually buried them.

It was a long, grim day, with the blizzard unre-lenting and the men, taking turns to keep warm in the single tent, gradually becoming covered in snow and merging into the landscape.

Pedler returned a few hours later, trying to find a landing place, but was defeated by the growing ferocity of the storm and had to go back to the ship. However, even later that day he courageously returned yet again, this time managing to land, and picked up the frozen, exhausted men.

Dangerously overloaded, the Mark 3 limped back to the *Antrim*, a red streak in the vast greyness, and dropped onto the swaying deck like a bloated fly too heavy to stay aloft. It was not a graceful touch-down, given the weight of the helicopter, but it was an exemplary display of skill and courage of the kind the SAS admired.

'Didn't even *see* an Argie,' Danny said wryly, trying to make light of the disaster. 'They must all be in England.'

That copped a few sour laughs.

5

'Let's face it, gentlemen,' the grim-faced OC of the Squadron said in the briefing room aboard the *Antrim*, now sailing for Stromness Bay, South Georgia, 'the whole Fortuna Glacier op was a total, humiliating disaster.'

'Sorry, boss,' Major Parkinson said, 'but I'm afraid I can't agree. The fact that two Naval helicopters crashed was due to the weather, not to our men. In fact our men showed exemplary courage, given what they endured.'

'Exemplary courage,' the OC replied drily, 'was also shown by the three Navy pilots, particularly Lieutenant-Commander Pedler. We can't take too much credit for that. Even worse, it was 42 Commando's second-in-command who warned us not to attempt it. Our mistake and humiliation, Major Parkinson. Let's admit it.'

'No, sir. The endurance displayed by our men

is already the talk of the whole fleet. In that sense, at least, it was a victory. I think we did well, sir.'

The OC grinned. 'Such loyalty!' Then he became serious again. 'Nevertheless, we can't let the matter rest here. We must have that reconnaissance. The recapture of South Georgia will be another turn of the screw as London tries to avoid the need for a full-scale assault on the Falkland Islands. Also, though it has no airfields, South Georgia represents a base much closer to the Falklands than Ascension Island – one where we can at least anchor our ships beyond the range of Argentinian fighter-bombers. If we can't manage an insertion by air, let's go in by sea.'

'I second that, boss,' said Boat Troop Captain Laurence E. Grenville. 'I believe we should launch our Gemini inflatables and try to set up OPs on the north-west of the island.'

'Naturally, you would,' Captain Hailsham said tersely.

'Well,' Grenville replied, 'the Fortuna Glacier is obviously out of the question, so we might as well try elsewhere, landing by sea.'

'I agree,' the OC said. 'We should try for Grass Island as a jump-off point to Leith and Stromness. If we can establish a couple of OPs there, we'll have compensated for the Fortuna

Glacier disaster. I suggest we take this action immediately – let's say this afternoon.'

'Right, sir,' Captain Grenville said, grinning impishly at Major Parkinson and Captain Hailsham. 'I'll get it organized right away.'

Hailsham grinned too, and held up his thumb, good-naturedly acknowledging Grenville's little *coup*. 'Who dares wins,' he said.

Grinning even more broadly, Grenville left the briefing room and made his way down through the many hatches and corridors of the swaying ship to the hold used for rest and mass briefings. There, he found Sergeant Ricketts, still exhausted from the previous day's ordeal, surrounded by the equally shattered members of the Mountain Troop and the still fresh, bantering Boat Troop.

'. . . and I maintain,' Danny was saying defensively, 'that . . .'

'Bullshit,' Gumboot interjected. 'No point blaming the bloody Navy. If you'd had men of calibre, like us, you'd have managed somehow.'

'Right,' Jock added. 'If they'd given the job to our Boat Troop, instead of you bullshit artists, we'd be sitting in an OP on that glacier right now – not thawing out our frozen dicks on this Navy brig.'

'The only bullshit artists here are the sods of the

Boat Troop,' big Andrew said, grinning at Danny, Paddy and Ricketts in turn, 'and right now the bullshit's flying like diarrhoea. You bastards can hardly row your fucking boats, let alone climb a glacier.'

Captain Grenville had been standing at the other side of the hatchway, just listening, amused, but he stepped forward when the good-humoured jeering and clapping of both sides had subsided. When he stepped into the recreation room, which the SAS were using as an all-purpose barracks, with bashas made up on the floor, the noise subsided even more.

'Sounds like bullshit from both sides,' Grenville said. 'At least you troopers are still awake. Anyway, if points are to be made, now's the time to make them. I've come to say we're going to try another insertion, this time by sea, in the hope of setting up an OP on Grass Island, about two miles from Leith. If you bullshit artists of the Boat Troop think you're better, now's your chance to prove it.'

After another outburst of hoots and catcalls, the former from the Boat Troop, the latter from the Mountain Troop, Ricketts, more serious than the others, asked: 'What are we supposed to be doing in the meantime?'

'You rest up and wait,' Grenville told him. 'Once we set up OPs, there's going to be a wide-scale assault on South Georgia. You'll all be involved in that.'

'Throwing snowballs,' Gumboot said, standing up with a wicked grin on his face. 'That's why you got in the Mountain Troop.'

The anticipated rejoinders flew thick and fast, until Captain Grenville silenced them all with his raised hand.

'OK, that's enough. I want all members of the Boat Troop to get kitted out immediately, then gather at the docking area. We're going to launch as soon as the Geminis are inflated. I'll see you down there in one hour. That's it, gentlemen. On your way.'

The members of the Boat Troop cheered and hurried out through the hatchway, leaving Ricketts and the rest of his exhausted team to thaw out and get some rest.

The docking area at the stern of the ship had been opened and was already being flooded when the men of the Boat Troop assembled near the launching bay. Kitted out with waterproof clothing and the usual array of weapons, the Boat Troop also carried special survival suits, life-jackets and

SARBE beacons, to facilitate the pick-ups and, if necessary, aid rescue from the sea.

The five Geminis to be used in the operation, already inflated and roped to the docking bay, were being lifted towards the men on the rising sea as it poured into the open stern to flood the bay area, rushing, roaring and spewing spray in every direction.

Seeing it from this vantage point, the sea appeared to slope up to the distant, stormy horizon, soaring and rolling dramatically in immense, shadowed waves that appeared to be about to swamp the ship, though they simply made it rise and fall as if made of cork. The sky was just as threatening, hanging low, filled with black clouds, and the wind that came rushing in to smack the men was icy and vicious.

'Looks like hell out there,' Grenville said. 'I think we're in for a rough time.'

'So let's go, boss,' urged Jock. 'We best go before nightfall.'

'Right, Corporal. Let's do it.'

The men embarked in the five Geminis, three to each boat, with Captain Grenville in charge of the lead craft, Gumboot, Taff and Jock sharing another. There were two large inflatables, powered by 40hp outboard motors, and three smaller versions, powered by 18hp motors, with the smaller ones roped to the larger ones – two to one, one to the other. When the docking ropes had been untied and the outboard motors turned on, the inflatables cruised out of the docking area, one after the other, and immediately were carried up and away on the giant swells of the windswept sea.

The immense waves picked the boats up, carried them through shrieking wind, above ravines of light-flecked darkness, then swept them back down into roaring, spinning tunnels formed by waves curling almost above them, threatening to swamp them. When low in the water, the waves pounded against the inflatables and washed over the men, pummelling them mercilessly and making a dreadful drumming sound against the rubber hulls. When raised on high, barrelling along the crest of the waves with the men glancing down what appeared to be dizzy depths of light and darkness, the outboard engines, coming clear of the water, shrieked and shook dementedly.

Within minutes the *Antrim*, which had been towering above them like a brightly lit skyscraper, receded into the stormy ocean, blending in with the grey haze where sea and sky merged, until little of it remained within view. Then it disappeared completely, leaving only the sea and sky, while the inflatables, rising and falling, plunging in and out of the water, shrieked and vibrated like wild things that could not be controlled.

In his smaller inflatable, roped to Captain Grenville's larger boat, Taff struggled with the rudder, trying to keep the boat close to the one ahead in case the rope snapped. It was a Herculean endeavour, requiring great physical strength, since the howling wind and raging, roaring water were relentlessly trying to hammer and tear it from his hand.

Jock McGregor and Taff Burgess were seated right in front of him, both leaning forward, heads bowed, stretched out over the strapped-down weapons and equipment. In charge of the waterproof PRC 319 radio, Jock was keeping in contact with Captain Grenville in the larger Gemini, which, a good distance ahead of them, kept disappearing in immense fountains of spray, then materializing again, often on the crest of giant waves. It seemed to float high above them, almost touching the black, tumultuous clouds, as if about to take wing.

'Christ, Taff!' Gumboot bawled back over his hunched shoulder. 'What the fuck are you doin' back there? This inflatable's like a bloody buckin' bronco! Keep control of that rudder!'

'Go screw yourself, Gumboot,' Taff shouted against the roaring wind. 'If I can't control this rudder, no one can – not in this bloody sea.'

'Excuses, excuses – always bloody excuses!'

'If I didn't have my hand on this rudder, I'd shove it right down your tonsils.'

'You and whose army?'

Jock knew that the banter was simply a healthy way of letting off steam at difficult times. All the same, their conversation was distracting and could cause him to miss something on the radio. Glancing up at the raging sea, observing the immense, curling waves and dark, boiling sky, he decided to tell them to shut up, to enable him to make a call to Captain Grenville in the Gemini ahead. Even now, this was being carried aloft on the crest of a wave, only to be swept down the other side, out of sight once more.

At that moment, the corporal in charge of the small boat roped to the other large Gemini cried over the radio: 'Damn it! Our outboard motor's cut out! It's not working, Captain!'

'We'll try to tow you,' said Captain Marsh of the other large Gemini, 'but in this kind of wind . . . Damn, the tow rope's already too taut. I don't think it'll hold.'

Glancing ahead and to the side, Jock saw the

rope that tied his own and another small inflatable to Captain Grenville's large Gemini. It was being given enough slack to hold because Taff, controlling the rudder, was also driving the outboard motor and trying to keep up with the boat ahead. However, with its engine dead, the other inflatable's tow rope had stretched as tight as it could go and looked to be on the point of snapping in two.

Jock felt he should warn them. His stomach heaved as, about to make the call, his own, smaller Gemini, roped to the one in front, followed its dizzying course up the next wave, then plunged down the other side, into barrelling darkness and the deafening roar of the churning sea.

When it emerged, the outboard motor had cut out.

'What the hell ...?' Taff bawled, furiously working the rudder, glancing back over his shoulder at the silent mechanism, which was smashing in and out of the water, but flapping about loosely. 'Fucking hell!' he exclaimed. 'The bastard's practically been torn off by the waves. We've no engine left, Jock.'

'Jesus Christ! What else?' Jock pleaded, glancing back at the smashed motor, then across the boiling, roaring sea just as the rope of the third small craft, being towed by the other big Gemini, snapped in two, with the two halves whipping up in the air like giant, crazed snakes, only to be slapped back down by the howling wind. Set free, the small inflatable, its outboard motor dead, went spinning away from the larger craft, completely out of control, then disappeared beyond a series of high waves. It did not reappear.

'Shit!' Gumboot exclaimed, his flinty eyes scanning the sea, fearlessly taking in all that was happening. 'I think we're fucked, mates.'

He was not far wrong. Even as Taff fought with the rudder and Jock checked the location of the boat ahead, the lack of an engine let the surging waves sweep their boat violently to the west, snapping the tow rope.

'We're adrift! Gumboot bawled.

Taff struggled with the rudder, trying to turn towards Captain Grenville's Gemini, but the loss of an outboard motor defeated him, giving the sea dominion. The inflatable was swept up on a wave, careered down the other side, miraculously survived a spinning tunnel of roaring water, then rushed farther westward. Grenville's Gemini soon disappeared, moving on towards Stromness and now hidden by the surging waves, while Taff, exhausted, struggling with his useless rudder, was forced to give up and let the raging sea take them where it would.

It took them towards Antarctica.

Captain Grenville watched the second dinghy disappear beyond the turbulent horizon with a deep feeling of shock. Now he was left with only one dinghy in tow, while the other large Gemini had none. He had just lost two boats and six good men, with little hope of getting them back. He could scarcely believe it.

Glancing in one direction, he saw only the raging sea and its soul mate, the cloud-black sky; glancing ahead he saw the jagged hills of Grass Island emerging out of the storm. He looked out to sea again, desperately hoping to spot the lost boats, but he saw only huge waves, one falling and breaking on the other with a terrible roar.

Praying to God that the men in the lost boats would be all right, though holding out little hope, he turned back to his own men and said, 'All right, we're still here, practically there, so let's make our insertion. That beach is only half a mile away and we're going straight onto it.'

The storm abated a little as they headed for the shore, but about 400 yards out, when the white, frozen hills were visible through the mist, snow started falling on them, as if to make up for the lessening wind. The men huddled up in their waterproof outfits and prepared for the landing.

Luckily, the closer they came to the shore, the less the wind blew and the more settled the formerly raging sea became. Slowing down their outboard motors, the pilots of the two large Geminis inched carefully into shallow waters, then stopped and anchored, enabling the men to clamber out and wade to the shore, carrying their light M16s above their heads.

'Leave the rest of the equipment in the boats,' Captain Grenville ordered. 'We may not be stopping here.'

Leaving his exhausted men on the beach, within sight of the inflatables bobbing out in shallow water, Grenville held his M16 at the ready and hurried up the snow-covered hill directly ahead. Reaching the summit, he was able to look across the small island to Leith Harbour, only two miles away. Blocks of ice were floating in the water, but the storm had abated. Glancing around him, Grenville saw nothing but other hills covered with snow and ice; there was no sign of Argentinian troops. Looking out to sea, he could not even see the British fleet; nor was there any sign of the two missing dinghies – only what now looked like calmer sea under a dark, stormy sky, from which snow was falling steadily. Satisfied, he returned to the men resting on the snow-covered, pebbled shore.

'There's no storm between here and Leith Harbour,' he said, 'so I think we should move on to South Georgia and set up our OPs. Let's do it now, before the storm reaches here or a new one starts up. Do you men think you're up to it?'

'Do birds sing?' one of the men asked. 'Do men shit? Of *course* we're up to it, boss.'

'That's the spirit, lads. So, let's get going.'

They returned to the boats, started the outboard motors and cruised around the small, bleak island. They then set off across the two miles of ice-filled water, heading straight for South Georgia. The sky was low and ominous, but the storm did not return, and the darkness, which had fallen with great speed, offered protection from Argentinian observation posts. Cruising slowly, quietly, between drifting blocks of ice, they managed to reach Stromness Bay without seeing, or even hearing, Argentinian patrol boats. However, just as Grenville was beginning to feel more confident, thinking his troubles were behind him, the blocks of ice gave way to drifting packs of gleaming, sharp ice splinters which punctured the inflatables, one after the other in rapid succession, causing the air to hiss out of them.

'Christ!' Captain Grenville exclaimed softly, then regained his sense of humour and said, 'OK, lads, abandon ship! Take everything but the rats.'

They were now only about thirty yards from the shore, in shallow, ice-filled water, which allowed them to clamber out of the hissing, sinking inflatables, form a chain from the boats to the shore, and pass the equipment along the human chain before the assault boats, crumpling pitifully, sank for good. Now, no matter what happened, they had no means of returning to the Fleet, hidden beyond the horizon.

Encircled by mountains that hid them from the Argentinians in Grytviken, they hid under an outcrop of rock until they had dried all of the equipment, shucked off their lifebelts, and were ready to march on in pursuit of locations suitable for observation posts.

'Since we can't get back to the fleet,' Grenville said, 'we'll just have to avoid the Argies and stay here until the assault begins. Bearing in mind that it can't begin until the fleet receives our recces, it's up to us to do the best we can and send back as much intelligence as possible.'

'Not much else to do around here,' a corporal said sardonically, 'so we might as well do that.'

'No belly dancers,' a trooper said. 'No strippers. No pubs full of beer. A man has to do something.'

'Then let's go,' Grenville said.

After checking his map for two areas of high ground overlooking Leith Harbour and Stromness Bay – though not so obvious that the Argentinians would expect to find them there – Grenville broke the remaining members of his troop into two separate units, one to establish an observation post in the hills above Leith, the other, his own, to establish one above Stromness. He then marched his own team up to his selected vantage point overlooking both areas, where they settled down to building their OP.

Thirty years earlier both areas had been whaling stations, boasting hundreds of workers, but now they were virtually deserted and, viewed from the wind-whipped, moaning hills, they revealed themselves as no more than a few scattered lights in the night's chill, occasionally moonlit, darkness.

Though sited on high ground to provide the best possible view of enemy activities and enable transmission of information back to base, the OP had to be dug into the earth to screen it from enemy eyes. In this instance, Grenville remained on guard and radio watch while his three troopers, using spades and pickaxes, dug the hole in which they would stay until the assault came.

Because Grenville had no idea when the assault from the fleet would take place, he anticipated a long stay here and therefore had the men dig a rectangular layout, rather than the short-term star shape. The spoil from their digging was removed in bergens and sprinkled unobtrusively over the ground a good distance from the OP. Once this had been done, the hole was lined with plastic sheets and the troops put up a hessian screen, with a poncho and overhead camouflage net, supported by wooden stakes, iron pickets, and chicken wire, and including a camouflaged entry and exit hole. When this business was completed, the troopers, wearing face veils and thick leather gloves, settled down in the OP, taking turns as telescope observer and sentry, as well as in the rest bays, with their kit-well, including the weapons, piled up in the middle.

From the completed OP Grenville's signaller was able to establish communications with the *Antrim*, thus enabling Grenville to inform his OC about what had happened to him and the others. In return, he was informed that one of the missing boats had been found by helicopter and the crew returned safely to the fleet. The other missing boat, containing Corporal Jock McGregor and troopers Taff Burgess and Gumboot Gillis, was still missing, its occupants presumed drowned.

Disturbed by that news, Grenville tried not to show it and instead encouraged his men to settle down to the business of observing Argentinian movements from their OP.

The wind howled eerily all night. The snow covered them like a blanket. Before long, they were cramped, cold and uncomfortable, boots wet, limbs numbed by constricted blood. For most it would have been a night in hell, but Grenville and his men had been trained for this.

'Yesterday afternoon,' Major Parkinson informed the OC of the Squadron, in the company of Captain Hailsham and Sergeant Ricketts in the OC's private cabin aboard the *Antrim*, now anchored with the other ships far north of South Georgia, 'an Argentinian submarine was observed reconnoitring the coastline of the island, almost certainly looking for signs of British landings.'

'Did they see anything?'

'We don't think so.'

'But some of our men are safely ashore.'

'Correct. Captain Grenville managed to make it with three of the Geminis, two large and one small, after which he divided the men into two groups to set up well-hidden OPs in Leith and Stromness. We're now in radio contact.'

'What about the submarine?'

'The first good news is that while searching for it in his helo, Lieutenant-Commander Pedler spotted one of the missing SAS inflatables and lifted its three men to safety.'

'Which men?'

'Corporal Woodward and troopers Blakely and Powell.'

'What about the inflatable?'

'Corporal Woodward ensured that it would sink before letting himself be lifted up. Both Woodward and Pedler have confirmed that it sank before they left the area.'

'Excellent. Any sign of the second lost inflatable?'

'No, boss. Either it sank or it's been blown clear of the island, into the southern ocean.'

The OC just nodded, revealing little emotion. 'And the Argentinian submarine?'

'According to Argentinian radio signals monitored by the *Endurance* while she was anchored in Hound Bay, the submarine recently landed reinforcements on the island, bringing the Argentinian garrison strength up to about 140 men.'

'That's useful information, Major Parkinson, but not too encouraging.'

'Then let me encourage you, boss. Not long before dawn, Pedler's helo spotted the submarine on the surface as she sailed over the shallows of Cumberland Bay, heading out to look for the British fleet. He straddled her with two depth-charges. Soon afterwards, she was attacked by the *Endurance*'s Wasp and the Lynx from the destroyer HMS *Brilliant*. Those helicopters forced the submarine to run for King Edward's Point, with her conning tower damaged and listing after being hit by missiles.'

'That's good news, certainly. A real setback for the Argentinians. Let's hope the blighter sinks before it reaches King Edward's Point or at least is incapacitated when it gets there, which will set them back even more.' The OC sipped some coffee, put his cup down, then glanced at the map pinned on the wall, showing South Georgia and the surrounding area, with Leith Harbour, Stromness Bay and Grytviken clearly marked. 'Twenty-four hours ago,' he continued, 'just before our ships scattered north, Major Sheridan gave his final orders for an immediate landing to seize Leith and Stromness, even though our recces there are incomplete.'

'A bit early, I'd have thought,' Parkinson said.

'And what do *you* think, Sergeant?' the OC, grinning slyly, asked Ricketts. 'I want to hear from the lower ranks.'

'I think he's keen to get his men ashore.'

'Why would that be?'

'Probably because there's been pressure from London to take the islands quickly.'

'For what reason?'

'As a further indication of Britain's political resolve. I think it makes sense, boss.'

'It's good to know that the lower ranks are well informed. Yes, Sergeant, it makes sense.' The OC smiled again, then glanced at the map of South Georgia. 'With the *Tidespring* still replenishing her tanks, M Company is six hours or more away from the coast. A landing force will therefore have to be improvised if we're to exploit the Argentinians' setback. In fact this has already been arranged between me and Major Sheridan. We're forming a quick reaction force of three composite troops aboard this very ship. Major Parkinson will lead the Mountain and remaining Boat troops; 2 SBS and the recce sections of

42 Commando will form a second composite troop; and the third troop will be made up from commando mortar-men and the ship's Marines.'

'That only comes to about seventy-five men,' Major Parkinson said. 'Scarcely more than half the strength of the Argentinian garrison.'

'You think the odds are too great?' the OC asked.

'Who dares wins,' Ricketts said.

After three days in his OP overlooking Stromness, Captain Grenville was virtually buried in snow, feeling as miserable as his SAS troop looked, but refusing to give in to self-pity and resolutely sending back to the fleet every scrap of information he had picked up on the movements of the Argentinians, both on land and out at sea, including the frequent submarine patrols out of Leith Harbour. This information had come from a combination of radio interception and visual observation, the latter either from foot patrols which went dangerously close to the Argentinian bases, to spy on them at close quarters, or by using binoculars to scan the sea from the hills. Either way, it was meticulously recorded and radioed back to the fleet under the most uncomfortable, dangerous circumstances.

The men, though now buried in snow, smelling their own shit and piss, increasingly frozen and exhausted, would hold out to the bitter end.

Like his men, Grenville was able and willing to hold out as long as necessary, but during the early afternoon of that third grim day, with the snow still falling on him, he was finding it difficult because of his concern for the three men still missing: Corporal Jock McGregor and troopers Taff Burgess and Gumboot Gillis – good men all, now almost certainly drowned because of the weather. Given the nature of the Fortuna Glacier fiasco, the way in which the other men had been lost was dreadfully ironic.

Determined not to give in to morbid thoughts, and to uphold the precepts of the SAS by sticking it out as long as possible, Grenville gazed over the piled-up snow of his OP to observe Grass Island and, beyond it, the vast, grey, empty sea, now dimly, eerily lit by early afternoon's pale sun.

Suddenly a series of fiery flickerings illuminated the horizon. Then the distant roar of the fleet's big guns made the whole OP shake. The first shells exploded far below, sending smoke billowing up from the lower slopes of Leith Harbour and Stromness Bay.

The assault had begun.

6

With the thunder of the *Antrim*'s two 114mm guns pounding in their ears, Major Parkinson and his men, including Captain Hailsham and Sergeant Ricketts, all in full battle kit, filed into the helicopters clamped to the ship's landing pads. Taking his seat between big Andrew and Baby Face, Ricketts strapped himself in, then glanced out through the rain-streaked window as the ship swayed and tilted to one side. The sea, which was full of deep swells, seemed very far below him. When he looked in the other direction, back towards the ship, he saw the big guns jolting each time they fired, wreathing the whole deck in smoke.

The combined bedlam of the helicopters and the guns was like the end of the world and became even worse when, with more noise and much shuddering, the holding clamps were released and the helicopters lifted off the deck. They ascended vertically, hovered above the landing pad, moved sideways to hover right above the sea, then headed for shore.

'About time,' Danny said, clutching his high-velocity M16A2 assault rifle and instinctively running his fingers over his webbing and 30-round box magazines. 'I'm dead keen to go and take out those Argies.'

'We're not taking anyone out,' Ricketts said. 'We're just trying to scare them. We want their surrender.'

'They made Royal Marines lie belly-down on the ground,' Danny replied, with the dulcet tones of a choirboy. 'What we want is their balls.'

'I'll second that,' Paddy said.

Even as the helos headed for the shore, the big guns of the *Antrim* and the *Plymouth* were continuing to pound in a relentless onslaught that would ensure the landing area and Brown Mountain, which dominated it, were clear of Argentinians. Looking across that short stretch of mottled sea, Ricketts saw the billowing columns of smoke where the shells were exploding.

'What a fucking noise,' Paddy said. 'We should have plugged up our ears.'

'Those guns sound like music to me,' big

Andrew replied as he jotted down more words in his notebook. 'I take heart from that sound.'

'More poetry, is it?' Paddy asked. 'More shite for the Imperial War Museum?'

'The true artist is rarely appreciated in his own time,' Andrew said, closing the notebook and slipping it into one of the zipped pockets of his jacket. 'My day will come.'

The shore was now rushing at them, pebbled, streaked with snow, with the shells exploding further inland, on the hills of Brown Mountain. Ricketts glanced westward, beyond the other two helicopters, to where sea and sky met, thinking bitterly of how Taff, Jock and Gumboot had been lost. Either they had drowned or were still drifting helplessly towards the Antarctic, in which case they would almost certainly freeze to death, after suffering hypothermia and frostbite. A hell of a way to go.

When he looked down, he saw the shore whipping out of view, to give way to the inland hills and valleys, mostly barren and brown, though brightened here and there by snow and frost. The ground was rushing up at him.

'We're coming in!' Major Parkinson shouted from up front. 'Prepare for the landing!'

The men unclipped their safety belts and

stood awkwardly in a metallic jangle of rifles, hand-grenades, bayonets, ammunition belts and water bottles. Burdened with bergens, bulky in their Gore-tex jackets, they resembled strange, hunchbacked animals. The helo shuddered as it slowed down, hovering right above the ground. The door opened with a screech as it descended, letting the cold air come howling in.

Major Parkinson was at the opening, standing beside Captain Hailsham, a radio-telephone held up to his ear, his free hand firmly gripping a support as the wind beat wildly at him, threatening to suck him out and spin him away like a twig.

As they approached the ground, the rotors whipped up dirt and snow, made foliage dance and bend, creating a minor hurricane that shook the whole helo. 'Go! Go! Go!' Parkinson bawled – and the first man disappeared through the opening before the helicopter had touched down. It did so as the second man went out and the queue inched towards the door. The helo was still bouncing lightly on its landing skis as Ricketts followed the others out, landing safely on the snowy, frosted ground.

He fanned out with the men already advancing, leaning forward to escape the drag of the whirlwind created by the helo's spinning, roaring rotors. The men all had their weapons at the ready, but there was no sign of enemy troops — only that desolate, rolling landscape, blanketed in snow and frost, viewed hazily through a white-gauze curtain of loose snow whipped up by the spinning rotors.

'Let's go! Move out!'

They were on the lower slopes of Hestesletten, a high valley located about a mile south-east of the former British Antarctic Survey buildings on King Edward's Point and separated from it by Brown Mountain. The sea surrounded them on all sides, flat and featureless from the heights, but the Fleet was now clearly visible, with its aircraft-carriers, destroyers, frigates, tankers and supply ships spread out as far back as the horizon.

The guns of the *Antrim* and the *Plymouth* were still firing, laying down a barrage that would methodically move forward to within 800 yards of the enemy position, the aim being to demoralize them rather than cause physical damage — a further ploy in the diplomatic war to recapture the Falklands. Plumes of smoke were still billowing up from the other side of Brown Mountain as the shells fell relentlessly around King Edward's Point.

'That's it,' Paddy said. 'Pound the shite out of

the bastards. Make 'em blind, deaf and dumb before we get there. Give them all diarrhoea.'

'Shut up, Paddy,' Ricketts said without malice. 'Come on, men, let's move out!'

The helos were already taking off again, whipping up more soil, stones and loose snow, as the men fanned out and started uphill, burdened under their bergens and carrying an assortment of firepower, including Heckler & Koch MPA3 sub-machine-guns, M16A2 assault rifles, 7.62mm self-loading rifles, Browning 9mm high-power handguns, 81mm mortars, fragmentation, white-phosphorus and smoke grenades, plus all the ammunition required for them. Also taken along were laser rangefinders, thermal imagers for night viewing, a couple of radios and, in the heavily loaded bergens, food, drink, toiletries and first-aid kits.

As the guns roared out at sea and shells exploded on the far side of Brown Mountain, filling the air beyond the summit with billowing clouds of smoke that dispersed under sullen clouds, the men marched uphill with weapons at the ready.

'We're being followed by the other composite troops being landed by boat,' Major Parkinson explained with the suppressed glee of an ageing officer who was having his last fling. 'The plan is to meet at the British Antarctic Survey buildings on King Edward's Point, so let's fan out and head for that very place.'

'Sure thing, boss,' Ricketts said, glancing back over his shoulder, down the slopes of the mountain, to see half a dozen landing-craft cutting a swathe through the sea as they surged away from the fleet, heading for the shore, under the protection of Sea King helicopters.

Glancing left and right, to where his men had fanned out along the frosty slopes of brown grass and stone, Ricketts saw the monolithic Trooper Andrew Winston – the only man who didn't appear dwarfed by his bergen and other equipment – striding fearlessly towards the crest of the mountain. Beside him, Baby Face Porter seemed very slight indeed, though he looked distinctly energetic, as he always did when properly engaged.

Proud of his men, Ricketts was also intrigued by them: touched by the poet hidden in Trooper Winston's huge body; just as he was amused by the gap between young Danny's naïvety when it came to his beloved Darlene, whom Ricketts thought was a tart, and his finely honed, assured killer's instincts when it came to warfare. 'Baby Face' indeed!

Then there was Corporal Paddy Clarke, who, barely educated and far from sophisticated, had never been known to make a mistake in action. He was one of the best of the SAS.

Ricketts studied them with pride, glad to be one of them, but inevitably they made him think of the men missing at sea – Gumboot Gillis and Taff Burgess, and Jock McGregor – and those thoughts, which were depressing, were also dangerously distracting and therefore had to be expunged ruthlessly from his mind, so that he could concentrate on the job at hand. The surrounding hills could be filled with Argentinian troops, so this was no time for mournful thoughts.

Out at sea, the big guns of the *Antrim* and the *Plymouth* were pounding away. More smoke was billowing up from beyond the summit of Brown Mountain, obviously rising from the explosions in the area of King Edward's Point and Grytviken, on the opposite side of the bay.

'Spread out even more!' Major Parkinson shouted, trying to make himself heard above the thunder of the big guns and the roar of the explosions. 'There could be mines in this area, so keep your eyes well peeled.'

They marched for another hour in a tense, watchful silence, relieved only by the booming of the guns out at sea and the explosions from the far side of the mountain. The hills they were crossing seemed devoid of all life, though the wind was constantly moving the sparse foliage, keeping the men on edge, aiming their weapons at anything that moved, ever ready to open fire.

When another hour had passed, Ricketts was practically yearning to engage the enemy, if only to find relief from this nerve-racking non-event of a march. Sometimes, when in action, he thought of his wife and children – as he was now doing occasionally – but mostly his thoughts drifted to previous engagements, the good and bad experiences they had given him – successful raids, disasters or the death of friends, like Lampton in Belfast. Such recollections were, at least, a way of staying focused on all the skills he had been taught, reminding him that the enemy could be all around him, watching him right now.

Glancing to his left, Ricketts saw the quick movement of tussocks of grass, followed by what appeared to be the rise and fall of a balaclava helmet. Without thinking twice, he called out a warning, dropped to his knees and let rip with a burst of gunfire from his M16A2. The noise was shocking, reverberating around the hills, and the tussocks of grass he had seen moving were torn apart by the bullets, exploding into the air.

A blood-curdling screeching was heard as the other men also opened fire. Ricketts jumped up and ran towards the enemy position, followed almost immediately by the other men. The inhuman sound continued, but no fire was returned as Ricketts and the others advanced, weapons at the ready, to where the remaining grass, now thrashing wildly, was soaked in fresh blood. They all studied the victim.

'Shit!' Andrew exclaimed.

'So *that's* what an Argie looks like!' Paddy said, grinning mockingly at Ricketts. 'Good one, Sarge!'

They had just shot an elephant seal, which was still screaming and writhing in agony in its own blood, its white ribs smashed and exposed through torn, flapping skin, its eyes wild with shock.

'Oh, God,' Ricketts said.

There was a sudden, short burst of fire from an M16 assault rifle and the seal shuddered violently, then was still.

Baby Face, who had fired the shots, stepped forward, gently kicked the seal with his boot, checking that it was dead, then stepped back again.

'Just putting it out of its misery,' he said, calmly checking his weapon. 'Only thing to do.'

'Yeah, right,' Paddy said after too long a silence.

'Let's move on,' Major Parkinson ordered, leading the way, now in sight of the summit of the hill and keen to get there. 'And if anything else moves, shoot it,' he added. 'We can't take chances, lads.'

In fact, though more than one elephant seal copped it by making a sudden movement and going down in a hail of bullets before the men finally reached the summit, no Argentinian troops were seen on the mountain range.

From the mountain's summit, through a curtain of smoke thrown up by the exploding shells of the fleet, they could see only what looked like a deserted settlement with white flags flying from several buildings – though the Argentinian flag still flew from its mast near the headquarters, formerly the British Antarctic Survey settlement, on King Edward's Point.

Most of the barrage had been laid down with air-burst shells, but other shells from the fleet had filled the hills above the rocky cove with ugly black holes. Nevertheless, the barrage had, as planned, been stopped before reaching the cove itself, leaving the white-walled, red-roofed buildings on King Edward's Point intact, as was the old whaling station of Grytviken on the opposite shore.

The Argentinian submarine damaged by AS 12 missiles had indeed managed to limp into harbour and was beached there, right in front of the untouched settlement.

'Those *are* white flags we're seeing, are they not?' Major Parkinson asked rhetorically.

'Yes, boss,' Captain Hailsham said. 'Looks like the big guns did the trick.'

'Let's find out,' Parkinson said. 'Signaller! Get in touch with Major Sheridan on the *Antrim*, then give me that phone.' The trooper in charge of the PRC 319 did as he had been told, then handed the telephone to Parkinson. When he had finished speaking to Major Sheridan, Parkinson handed the phone back and turned to Hailsham and Ricketts. 'Excellent. Sheridan's already been in contact through the *Antrim*'s radio with the Argentinian headquarters in the Survey buildings and they've confirmed that they're eager to surrender. However, they also warned that there are minefields laid in defence of their weapon pits.'

'Then I suggest we go in via the shore,' Captain Hailsham said. 'As their submarines have been moving in and out of there, we can assume they won't have mined that area.'

'Right.' Parkinson turned to Ricketts. 'Move the men down to the shore, Sergeant. Ensure that they don't get trigger-happy. If the Argies emerge with their hands up – as I think they will – let them come out in one piece.'

'Yes, boss. Will do.'

Ricketts called the men together and told them what was happening. 'So keep your fingers off the triggers,' he added, 'if they come out with their hands up.'

'Politics!' Paddy said in disgust, then spat on the ground.

'If I step on a mine going down there,' big Andrew said, 'I want you guys to take that settlement apart.'

'That's a *British* settlement,' Danny reminded him. 'That's why the fleet didn't shell it.'

'Very kind of them, I'm sure. I bet the Argies are real pleased. We lost at least three men out on that sea while those Argie bastards sat down there laughing.'

'Bullshit,' Ricketts said, staring up at Andrew's angry brown eyes. 'The fact that we lost three men at sea isn't an issue here. This isn't the bloody Boy Scouts, Trooper – it's the SAS – and any of you could cop it at any time, which is no cause for bitching. It's just part of the job.'

'Yes, boss.'

'Let's go.'

Led by Parkinson and Hailsham, they marched across hills pock-marked by scorched shell holes, high above the settlement, then went carefully downhill towards the shore, keeping their eyes peeled for buried mines. No mines went off, no one was hurt, and just as they reached the shore and were advancing on the tall radio towers in front of the settlement, Argentinian soldiers started emerging from the buildings, a few waving white flags, the others raising their hands in the air.

'Looks like you were right, boss,' Ricketts said.

'Yes,' Parkinson replied. 'Surrender it is.'

Even as some of the SAS troop fanned out to surround the Argentinians and keep them under cover, others entered the buildings to check for snipers and booby traps.

'Not too impressive, are they?' Paddy mused, studying the unshaven, frightened men coming out of the buildings with their hands raised. 'They look like a bunch of fucking schoolkids.'

'They're mostly conscripts,' Andrew explained. 'Not professional soldiers. Most of them didn't even want to fight this war. The poor sods were forced into it.'

'My heart bleeds for them,' Paddy said.

'Mine doesn't,' Danny said. 'You don't put Royal Marines on the ground and then take bleedin' photographs.'

'I shudder to think what this kid would be feeling,' Paddy said to Andrew, 'if those Royal Marines had been SAS troopers.'

'If they had been,' Andrew replied, indicating the prisoners with a nod of his head, 'these poor bastards wouldn't be alive right now. Danny Boy would have slaughtered them.'

'Yeah,' Paddy said, 'I believe he would have.'

Parkinson and Hailsham, carefully covered by Ricketts, Andrew, Paddy and Danny, advanced to meet the Argentinian captain walking cautiously towards them beside a corporal holding a makeshift, wind-blown white flag. The officer wasn't young and he carried himself with quiet dignity. When he reached Parkinson, his back stiffened and he saluted. Parkinson returned the salute.

'Captain Bicain,' the Argentinian said in good English, introducing himself. 'As Commander of this garrison, I wish to formally offer our surrender.'

'Thank you, Captain,' Parkinson replied. 'I accept your surrender on a temporary basis. The formal acceptance will take place tomorrow when more British troops, including my superiors, fly into Leith. In the meantime, we'll look after your men and treat you with respect.'

'Of course,' Captain Bicain said with some pride and a distinct touch of arrogance. 'Why not? We have only been performing our duty in this little gesture.'

'A little gesture?' Parkinson asked. 'This is a war!'

Captain Bicain smiled, shrugged, and shook his head in denial. 'A war? No, Captain, it was merely a gesture. *El gesto de las Malvinas* – the Falklands gesture. That's what we call it in Argentina, and that's what it is. This is no real war, Captain.'

'Call it what you will,' Parkinson replied, his cheeks reddening with anger, 'but please consider yourself a prisoner of war – as are all of your troops. For the time being, at least until the others arrive, we'll return you to your quarters and keep you under guard. Hopefully you'll be shipped out tomorrow.'

'Thank you,' Captain Bicain said, kicking his heels and saluting again. He was then marched away by Captain Hailsham and two SAS troopers, disappearing into the building from which he had just emerged as Parkinson's men surrounded the other, less proud Argentinians.

'A gesture!' Parkinson exclaimed in disgust. 'I suppose that will ease the national conscience – not war: a mere gesture. Pretty neat, yes?'

He was addressing Captain Grenville, who merely grinned. 'Come on, Captain,' Parkinson said, 'let's investigate this settlement thoroughly. Our job isn't finished yet.'

'Yes, boss, let's do that.'

They were just about to march off when a Lynx helicopter descended, whipping up a wind that beat wildly at them and filled the air with flying pebbles. It landed on the shore near the radio antennae.

Jock, Taff and Gumboot jumped out of the helicopter, whooping gleefully and raising their M16s above their heads. The rest of the troop, getting over their surprise, let out a mighty cheer.

'Drowned at sea?' Gumboot said, standing with Taff and Jock, surrounded by his mates, and studied mournfully by the defeated Argentinians. 'You gotta be joking, mate!'

'After being blown westward for a bit,' Taff explained, 'thinking we'd end up in Antarctica, we managed to wade ashore on the north coast of Stromness Bay, about four kilos from our intended landing point.'

'We've been there for the past three days,' Jock added, 'freezing our nuts off, but maintaining radio silence so as not to fuck up this operation. Then, when you lot landed, we sent out a SARBE radio signal and got picked up by the helo.'

'I know you lot were secretly *hoping* we'd copped it,' Gumboot said with a wide grin, 'but unfortunately for you, here we are, fit and rarin' to go.'

'And still good with the bullshit,' Ricketts said, grinning. 'OK, men, let's get back to work. I want all the Argentinian weapons collected and laid out here on the ground. Then search the Argies and bed them down for the night. We've no time to listen to Gumboot's tall tales. We've got a long wait ahead of us.'

Laughing, unable to hide their delight, the men either patted Gumboot, Taff and Jock on the back or more formally shook them by the hand, before going back to the job in hand.

The enemy weapons were collected and piled up in front of the HQ, the Argentinians were searched, locked up and kept under guard in the settlement buildings, and the SAS settled down to wait for the arrival of the men from the landing-craft.

Next morning, when the replacements had arrived, SAS and SBS teams flew into Leith and formally accepted the surrender of its garrison.

The Argentinian flag was lowered and the White Ensign was soon fluttering alongside the Union Jack, over Grytviken.

'South Georgia's been recaptured,' Major Parkinson announced proudly to his men. 'Now it's on to the Falklands.'

7

While D Squadron, under the temporary command of Captain Hailsham, were finishing off
their task in South Georgia, Major Parkinson
and Captain Grenville of the Boat Troop were
flown out on a 772 Naval Air Squadron Wessex
Mark 5 to join G Squadron on the fleet replenish-
ment ship, the 22,890-ton Royal Fleet Auxiliary
Resource.

The RFA *Resource* had a helicopter flight deck
from which troopers could be flown to other
ships, including HMS Hermes, now leading the
naval battle group towards the Falklands. It was
not unusual, therefore, that when the Wessex
Mark 5 came in to land, other matt olive-drab
helicopters were circling above, also waiting to
land, while the Royal Naval Squadron ground
crew and frantic flight-deck parties busily loaded
the helos, either by hand or with jackstay rigs.

After disembarking onto the noisy, seemingly chaotic flight deck, high above the stormy sea, Parkinson and Grenville were met by Navy Chief Petty Officer Ken Brown who guided them through the ship's labyrinthine corridors and hatchways to the surprisingly large briefing room. There they partook of tea and sandwiches while Lieutenant-Commander Chris Holdfield of Naval Intelligence and Lieutenant-Colonel Adrian Granthorpe of SAS Intelligence, the much-maligned 'green slime', discussed their plans for the invasion of the Falkland Islands.

'How can we be sure that we won't reach an agreement with the Argentinians?' was Parkinson's first question. 'Now that we've recaptured South Georgia, they just might capitulate.'

'No, they won't,' Lieutenant-Colonel Granthorpe replied. 'They're now in too deep to back out with dignity. Neither the recapture of South Georgia nor any kind of diplomacy will be enough to get the Argentinians to voluntarily hand back the islands. We've checked this with Whitehall and they agree. It's just not going to happen.'

'I see,' Parkinson said, surprisingly guilty at how pleased he felt to know that conflict was coming. 'So what are you planning?'

'First, we use the whole fleet as a threat to

the occupation forces,' Lieutenant-Commander Holdfield informed him, 'then we put a landing force ashore.'

'Which is where we come in.'

'Correct,' Granthorpe said. 'However, before any landing can be made, we need to know the exact disposition of the Argentinian garrison's defences. So far we've assessed most of them to be dug in around Port Stanley, with the heaviest concentration facing south-west to prevent an advance along the road from Fitzroy. Unfortunately, that's about all we've managed to confirm so far.'

'No aerial or satellite pictures available?' Parkinson asked.

'None. And most of their defences are well camouflaged. For this reason, what we now require is good, old-fashioned, eyeball recces, for which we think the SAS and SBS are ideally suited.'

'Deep-penetration raids.'

'Exactly. These should cover not only the two main islands of East and West Falkland, but also some of the smaller islands around the coastline.'

'That's a lot of coastline,' Captain Grenville pointed out. 'Approximately '15,000 kilometres.'

'The SBS has spoken,' Granthorpe said with a smile. 'Was that an observation or a complaint?'

'Purely an observation.'

'I'm delighted to hear it.' Granthorpe turned to Major Parkinson. 'What are your problems?'

'The two main islands,' Parkinson replied, 'have a total area nearly equivalent to that of Wales, with a terrain like Dartmoor – windswept, rough pasture, no trees. However, there are many bogs and rock runs of slippery, moss-sided boulders, which in some runs are a metre or more across. To make matters worse, although the hills along the northern half of East Falkland rise to only 450 metres on Mount Kent, their climate is like that on English hills of twice that height. I think even the Special Forces will have a considerable problem in surviving in such conditions for lengthy periods of time – let alone doing so without being detected by the Argentinians.'

'This won't be made any easier,' Grenville added, 'by the fact that the Argentinians, at least according to our intelligence reports, are still in fighting spirit and have effective radio direction-finding equipment. They could use those to pick up our signals and locate the whereabouts of our OPs.'

'That's a chance you'll have to take,' Granthorpe replied. 'It's imperative that we reconnoitre all areas dominated by the enemy on East Falkland. We also have to maintain close observation of the garrisons on West Falkland.'

Lieutenant-Commander Holdfield jabbed his finger at the large map pinned to the board behind him. 'The latter lies 20 kilometres to the north, across Falkland Sound from the eastern island. Not too great a distance between them. In broad terms, therefore, the plan is to land on East Falkland sufficiently far from Port Stanley's airfield and large garrison, to enable a beachhead to be established before it can be heavily counter-attacked. From there, the main thrust of the attack will cross the mountains, where, as we believe, the Argentinians won't be expecting any major force. Once across these uplands, the back door to Stanley will be open.'

'Then let's kick it open,' Parkinson said. 'I'll arrange to fly my men out from South Georgia to the fleet and then land them from here.'

'Thank you, Major. Good luck.'

Chief Petty Officer Ken Brown led Parkinson and Grenville to the radio room, where with visibly mounting enthusiasm, Parkinson got in touch with South Georgia and issued instructions for the Squadron to be flown out. After receiving personal confirmation from Captain Hailsham, he switched off the microphone, turned to face Captain Grenville, and raised his thumb triumphantly. Grenville did the same, grinning lopsidedly, then he and Parkinson were led out of the radio cabin by Brown who, once he had them in the corridor, turned back to face them.

'So where do we make our HQ?' Parkinson asked him.

'Well, sir . . .' Chief Petty Officer Brown tried to hide a helpless grin by coughing into his fist. 'Actually, the only location I could find was the presently unused ladies' toilet?'

Parkinson stared steadily at him for a moment, then asked, as if deaf: 'Did you say the ladies' toilet?'

'Yes, sir,' Brown replied, now grinning openly. 'Sorry, but it's the only available room.' He spread his hands in the air in an expansive gesture. 'It's big, sir, believe me. Lots of space in there. We've already installed radios, and tables and chairs. Even a hot-drinks machine — soup, coffee and tea. If you need anything else, just ask. I think you'll be happy there.'

'You think this is funny, Petty Officer?'

'Absolutely not. No, sir!'

'Then get that grin off your face and take us to see it.'

'Of course. This way, sir.' Still grinning, the Chief Petty Officer led them through a hatchway, down a couple of flights of stairs, and through a dimly lit, smoke-filled hold filled with half-naked troops resting on tiers of bunks, in a tangle of clothing and equipment, to another corridor. The ladies' toilet was located at the end of it. 'This is it, sir,' Brown said, opening the door and waving them in.

Parkinson stepped in first, followed by Grenville and Brown, and thoughtfully studied the room. It was indeed surprisingly large, with a row of cubicles along one wall, a radio system resting on a bench against the opposite wall, a couple of portholes to one side, giving a view of the sea, and three folding tables, placed together in the middle, surrounded by hard chairs. A blackboard on a stand had been placed equi-distant between the portholes, with a map of the Falkland Islands and tide charts already pinned to it.

Parkinson nodded. 'I'm impressed, Petty Officer. I think this should be sufficient unto our needs. So where do we sleep?'

'In cabins in the officers' quarters, sir. Back

126

where we came from. You'll find your name on the door and the key in the lock.'

'You have thieves aboard this ship, Petty Officer?'

'Nothing is perfect under the sun or moon. In truth, the odd item goes missing, sir.'

'The SAS don't steal from each other. Perhaps you should join us.'

'That's a very kind invitation, sir, but I'm not as young as I used to be.'

Parkinson smiled at that. 'Very good, Petty Officer. I'm sure we can find our way back to our cabins. Your responsibilities end here.'

'Thank you, sir. My pleasure.'

Still grinning, the Chief Petty Officer departed, leaving Parkinson and Grenville alone in the room. Now also both smiling, they studied the room, then faced one another.

'So, what do you really think?' Grenville asked.

'I think it's fine,' Parkinson said. 'If nothing else, it should feed a few fantasies. Let's go up on deck.'

Leaving the ladies' toilet and closing the door, they made their way back along the corridor, through the hold filled with troops, and back up a series of ladders to the helicopter flight deck, where other troops were being cross-decked and helos being loaded with the aid of bright-yellow jackstay rigs. Other ships, including destroyers and aircraft carriers, were spread across the stormy sea to form a great armada, with aircraft taking off and landing constantly, flying between the airborne helicopters with breathtaking precision.

'Modern warfare,' Parkinson said to Grenville, 'is truly spectacular.'

'They don't make movies like this any more,' Grenville replied. 'Their budgets won't wear it.'

'I'm going to miss it, Laurence.'

'Yes, boss, I'm sure you will.'

Gripping the wet railing, letting the beating spray soak his face, Parkinson surveyed the scene with a helpless feeling of loss, remembering that his time with the SAS would soon be up, putting an end to the most exciting and challenging days of his life.

Coming to the SAS, like his father-in-law, from the Durham Light Infantry, he had taken part in the assault on the Jebel Akhdar in Oman in 1959, when he was only 22; organized a series of cross-border raids in Borneo in 1964, served in Northern Ireland throughout the troubled 1970s, and even helped orchestrate the daring rescue during the Iranian Embassy siege of 1980. Those were adventures a man didn't easily forget.

A military man by inclination as well as upbringing, he had a restless personality, needed constant distraction and could imagine no life outside the Regiment. Yet at 44, age was catching up with him, his time with the Regiment was running out, and unless something unexpected turned up elsewhere, this would almost certainly be his last engagement. With luck, he might be given a desk job back in England, in the Intelligence Corps at Stirling Lines, but even that wasn't guaranteed – and other options were limited.

The thought of an administrative position, shuffling papers instead of men, endorsing plans instead of making them, filled Parkinson with immeasurable gloom. Nor was he thrilled by the notion of taking early retirement and tending the garden of his house in Hereford, attractive though it was.

Even at his age, he now realized, he was not a man cut out for a 'normal' life. So, as he gazed at the ships spread out on the stormy sea, at the roaring planes and helicopters, he accepted that he was where he belonged and would not enjoy leaving it. Thank God for this campaign.

'I think the use of four-man patrols,' Parkinson said to Captain Grenville, needing to distract himself from his thoughts, 'is the best way to recce East and West Falkland. Insert on both islands and disperse the groups in all directions, marching by night to predetermined locations for the individual observation posts. Staying as long as necessary. Radio silence to be maintained until they've done all they can do and need lifting out. With so many small groups scattered all over, the chances of being caught are much reduced and the amount of intelligence gathered should be greatly increased. Naturally, the assault will only begin when that intelligence is gathered and assessed.'

'I agree,' Grenville said.

'The Squadron arrives tomorrow morning. In the meantime, while we're waiting, we can study those maps in the ladies' toilet and select the best places for the OPs. Let's go back down, Laurence.'

'Might as well get started,' Grenville replied. 'No point standing up here all day.'

Parkinson could happily have stayed up there all day, watching the aircraft, helicopters, destroyers and carriers, but he knew that it would do him little good, apart from making him sadder. So, after taking one last, fond glance at the fleet, he sighed and followed Captain Grenville back into the ship, down into its labyrinth of hatchways and corridors and holds, past the hundreds of troops resting in tiers of steel bunks, smoking and reading and playing cards and writing letters, in dimly lit holds smelling of sweat and stale, smoke-filled air. They made their way through it all to the smaller, cleaner, much brighter ladies' toilet, where the SAS HQ was now formally located.

There, compelled to smile at their lot, they unpinned the maps on the blackboard, spread them out on the tables and proceeded to plan the Squadron's deep-penetration raids on East and West Falkland.

8

The least exciting, but most demanding and valuable, of all SAS operations is the setting up and maintaining of observation posts by four-man patrols for recces inside enemy territory.

Chosen as the Patrol Commander, or PC, on the Squadron's transfer from South Georgia to the *Resource*, Ricketts was allowed to select his own team. He chose three men with the required specialist skills for this particular job: Corporal Paddy Clarke, Trooper Danny Porter, and the big black poet, Trooper Andrew Winston.

Unable to conduct the normal rehearsal phase because they were aboard ship, Major Parkinson instead briefed his team with the aid of maps and aerial photos taken from previous aircraft reconnaissance flights. Ricketts was then given a day to prepare the patrol, make his own plan of operations based on the briefing and tell the other three what was expected of them. He then chose, and supervised the inspection of, the required equipment and weapons, ensuring that radios and batteries were working, ammunition was clean, grenades were primed, rations were drawn and water bottles were filled. The weapons, of which there were a considerable number and variety, were individually tested by being fired at the turbulent sea from the wind-blown deck of the ship.

When this was completed, the members of the patrol were flown in on two 845 Squadron Wessex Mark 5 helicopters, which carried them the 125 miles from the *Resource* to the LZ near the centre of East Falkland. The night flight took them over the misty north-west coast of the island, then through a high-ridged, moonlit valley that led to the uplands. Wearing his Passive Night Goggles, or PNGs, which enabled him to see in the dark, even if only in shades of dream-like blue, the pilot had no difficulty in landing them on the correct LZ. Nevertheless, he did not touch down for long.

Though the idea had been to land a long way from Port Stanley, to avoid contact with the enemy, then march for two or three days to the chosen site of the OP, there was still a real danger of being seen. The pilot therefore hardly touched the ground, but mostly hovered a couple of feet above it as the SAS team jumped down and offloaded their kit. While they were doing this, Danny moved away from the LZ to act as sentry, his M16A2 assault rifle held at the ready. When the kit had been offloaded, the men hurried out of the whirlwind created by the spinning rotors and Ricketts waved the helo away. It ascended vertically, all its lights dimmed, and soon disappeared in the cloudy night sky.

For the rest of this first night no words would be spoken. Instead, Ricketts ordered his men forward with the use of hand signals. Similar signals became the sole means of communication throughout the long, dangerous march, which took them along the valley, then over the hills, skirting around the frost gleaming in the moonlight, always on the lookout for mines. The wind moaned eerily around them, shaking the sparse vegetation, making it difficult to hear the sounds that would have warned them of Argentinian patrols. Everything that moved or made a sound was a potential enemy.

Using an illuminated compass, and aligning landmarks and roads with the map to follow their pre-set route, they moved along in file formation with young Danny well in front, taking the 'point' as lead scout and constantly checking what lay ahead through the night-sight of his rifle. The other three were strung out behind him, a good distance apart, maintaining irregular space between them to avoid unnecessary, or too many, casualties if attacked.

Marching behind Danny, Ricketts as PC was second in line, with Paddy Clarke third as signaller and big Andrew bringing up the rear as 'Tail-end Charlie'. As lead scout, Danny's job was to cover an arc-shaped area in front of the patrol. Ricketts and Paddy covered arcs to the left and right respectively, while Andrew had to regularly swing around to face the direction from which they had come, not only covering their rear but also ensuring that the patrol had no blind spots. Each man had to constantly look left and right for signs of enemy movement, as well as check repeatedly that the men in front and behind him were still in place. It was a rigorous, demanding routine that could not be ignored.

Added to the mental strain of being constantly alert while not allowed to speak, was the sheer physical burden imposed by the extra weight the men had to carry on this particular patrol. Each of their bergens now contained extra link belts, magazines, explosives and other ammunition; spare radios or replacement parts and batteries; rations and water; a sleeping bag and spare clothing. Even more demanding were personal kit belts laden with additional survival gear, medical equipment, water bottles, emergency rations, and smoke and fragmentation grenades. Together, the bergens, kit belts and extra weapons made up a load that would have broken most men's backs on a hike such as this.

Nevertheless, tough as it was, to Ricketts there was a sublime logic and beauty in the very concept of the four-man patrol. Conceived by David Stirling, the creator of the SAS, the four-man patrol was the basic building block of the Regiment, a self-contained unit within a Sabre squadron, and one dependent on the absolute, unwavering trust between each of its members. This was one of its salient features. Another was the fact that though each member of the patrol had been given Cross-Training, to enable him to be proficient in all SAS skills, for the purposes of the four-man patrol each had his specialist role: in this instance, Danny as scout and tracker, big Andrew as linguist and medic, Paddy as signaller and demolitions expert, and Ricketts as PC, which required the ability to take over any of the other specialist roles should one of the men be wounded or killed. The four-man patrol was, then, a microcosm of the whole SAS – and an almost perfect, self-sustaining unit into the bargain.

Now, marching across the hills of central East Falkland, Ricketts felt a great pride that overruled his simmering frustration at the patrol's lack of progress. Because of the constant threat of contact with enemy foot patrols or of being seen by helicopters with electronic aids or solar imagers, as well as the need to always be on the alert for mines, progress was agonizingly slow.

By dawn the next day, though they had neither seen nor been in contact with the enemy in any form, they had covered only ten miles.

'We'll have to hide during the day,' Ricketts said, finally able to speak because dawn was breaking through the mist wreathing the distant, brooding hills and the grey sea beyond. 'So make yourselves a scrape and climb into it. Danny and Andrew will sleep first. You and me, Paddy, we'll rest next. Two hours on and two off for each man. OK, lads, get at it.'

'Right, boss,' Paddy said, clearly relieved he could talk at last and continuing to do so as he unstrapped his short-handled spade. 'I don't mind waiting my turn. Very sensible to let the babies rest first. You can tell the poor shites are already worn out and in need of their sleep.'

'Beauty sleep,' Andrew replied, digging his spade into the hard, frozen soil. 'When you're born black and beautiful, like me, you've a moral responsibility to remain that way. So it's beauty sleep, you ugly little bastard. That's all I need it for.'

'If you're beautiful, I'm a fucking orang-utan.'

'Who's arguing?' Andrew asked.

'Just shut up and dig,' Ricketts said. 'We haven't got all day, lads.'

'Hard at it, boss,' Danny said, digging the soil out with his spade and throwing it over his frail shoulder. 'It'll be done in no time.'

The 'scrape' is a small hollow scraped or dug out of the ground and covered with wire, which is then strewn with local vegetation. It is a temporary measure used for short-term rest by day or night, in the lying-up position, or LUP, which is actually *any* position chosen by the patrol.

In this case the men only dug, or scraped, hollows deep enough to stretch out in – two to sleep under the camouflaged roof of wire and turf, the other two to keep watch, with these functions being swapped every two hours.

It made for a long, wet, cold and miserable day in which psychological as well as physical strength was vital. Nor could they eat properly, since they dare not light a fire or use their hexamine stove; instead, they could only sustain themselves with snacks of cheese, biscuits and chocolate.

Having been particularly well trained in combating the torments of the mind, as well as those of the body, Ricketts and his men, while not especially liking the scrapes, took them in their stride and managed to survive an interminable day, during which they saw only the occasional Argentinian helicopter or aircraft, but no foot patrols.

By nightfall, they were on their way again, on another long march through dark countryside.

Inevitably, as they neared Port Stanley, they began to see, if not Argentinian troops, at least their positions, from the camp-fires glowing eerily in the darkness. When this happened, they recced that area and kept a record of the information, but did not radio it back to the fleet, for fear that the signal might be picked up by the enemy, leading to their location.

Occasionally they saw enemy foot patrols moving, like them, through the moonlit, misty darkness. When this happened they always dropped to the ground and kept the enemy under cover. But they didn't open fire, since their first objective was reconnaissance, not combat, and an engagement, even if won, would have blown their cover to enemy intelligence, thus jeopardizing the forthcoming assault. Though the temptation to open fire was very strong, they never gave in to it.

If the first day had been bad, the second was even worse. They could do little but hide in their scrapes until darkness fell again, either sleeping or keeping their eyes peeled for signs of enemy activity. Their psychological training was such that they were able to do this, though all of them did it in different ways.

Phil Ricketts was married and the father of two children, Julia, 10, and Anna, 11. His wife, Maggie, came from Wood Green, North London, was working-class and proud of it. She was a secretary in a mortgage company in the high street, and was independent, sensual and good-humoured. While the marriage was secure and Ricketts truly loved his wife, he was sometimes disturbed by the fact that he preferred a man's life, away from home and hearth, doing what only men could do. This wasn't gambling or getting drunk or screwing around; it was simply the need for adventure and the sharpened sense of life offered by constant danger.

Before joining the Army, Ricketts had worked as a toolpusher on the North Sea oil rigs. Though it was hard, dangerous work, he had always enjoyed being out there more than being at home. Some men are like that – they can't lead a normal life – and when Ricketts finally accepted that he was one of that breed, he sensibly enlisted in the Army.

At first Maggie had resented it, wondering what she had done wrong, but when she realized that he simply loved doing a man's job – that no other woman was involved – she let him get on with it.

Soon, not satisfied with routine work for the Army, Ricketts had applied to join the SAS. Once accepted, he knew he had found his real home. Nevertheless, when he was in an OP or, as now, in a scrape, trying to combat the silence and interminable hours of inactivity, he did it by dwelling on his marriage and why it wasn't enough for him. He had yet to find an answer to all his questions, but thinking about them helped pass the time.

Like Ricketts, young Danny also thought about his home life, though his thoughts ran along simpler lines. Danny had never harboured a doubt about what he wanted to do in life: from childhood, he had wanted to be a soldier – something both of his parents fully understood. He had collected toy soldiers, read war books, watched war movies, played soldiers instead of cowboys and Indians, then started collecting guns. In this sense, he had been a soldier since he was a boy; it just took time to get there.

Danny had always been small and slim, rather quiet and good-natured, but his temper was legendary during his school years and led him into a lot of fights. By the time he left school, at 15, he had decided that he wanted to join the Army and would let nothing stop him. Before he joined, when he was 18, he already knew that eventually he would transfer to the legendary SAS – which he did, passing every test. When at last he was awarded the winged dagger, he was not in the least surprised.

Nevertheless, Danny's confidence in his ability as an SAS trooper was not matched by the same in his personal life. Born and bred in the Midlands, he was the only child of decent, working-class parents who showered a great deal of affection on him and would have been surprised, even shocked, to learn of his violent temper and frequent fist-fights.

Though the fights were real enough, Danny, on leaving school, was too obsessed with getting into the Army to learn about life's other realities, notably sex. Inexperienced with girls, he viewed them too romantically; so, when he first met Darlene in the company of some mates and their girlfriends in a local pub, he could not resist the knowledge that she fancied him and was not shy of showing it.

He loved Darlene desperately, though with certain residual doubts, most based on idle gossip from those very same mates who had intimated that her father was a boozing prat, her mother a tart, and that she, Darlene, was inclined the same way. Though Danny had tried to ignore such comments, which wounded him deeply, they kept coming back to stain his pure love with the shadow of doubt.

So, when in an OP, or LUP in his scrape, Danny wrestled with the gulf between his total confidence as a member of the Regiment and his doubts when it came to personal matters.

Nevertheless, he only did so with one half of his brain, while the other half – always alert and with natural killer's instincts – never failed to concentrate on the job in hand.

Andrew and Paddy had very different kinds of

thoughts, which were, in both cases, much less personal. Though not quite a born killer like Baby Face, big Andrew had remarkable physical strength and, like Ricketts, an unappeasable hunger for excitement. All brute energy on the one hand, he was highly imaginative on the other, and needed to express both aspects of himself to prevent his boiler from bursting. His poetry expressed the inner self – that gentle soul in the enormous body – and the SAS, with its discipline and challenges, took care of the physical side.

Also, as the SAS took no account of his black skin, but judged him purely on his merits, Andrew felt as natural in the Regiment as he did when expressing himself through his poetry.

Not married and not planning to be – at least not yet – he passed the interminable time in OPs or, as now, in his cramped, damp scrape, by dreaming up more lines of poetry about his life with the Regiment.

Though he never forgot – not for one minute, second even – exactly why he was lying in silence in a hole in the ground. It was see or be seen, kill or be killed. He couldn't afford to forget that.

And Paddy? He had no problems. He didn't care if he lived or died. He'd lost both his parents in childhood, in a routine car accident in Merseyside, and been brought up by distant relatives, decent but dull. Fleeing at an early age, he had hitchhiked to London, became a labourer on a building site, drank too much, screwed around too much and routinely squandered his money. Drifting into petty crime, he had kicked a few heads and been kicked in turn, but eventually, after a spell in the nick, he had decided to call it a day. Seeing a TV ad that sold the Army as an adventure, he enlisted and ended up in Belfast, being assaulted with bricks, screamed at by housewives and occasionally fired upon by teenage snipers.

To his surprise, he loved it. The excitement made him whole. Born in Liverpool, he had never felt Irish, so had no problems in Belfast, Londonderry, or even in so-called 'bandit country', where he ambushed terrorists and was in turn ambushed, surviving it all. The 'enemy' was the one he was told to fight, and that's all there was to it.

Posted back to England, he found Army life dull, so decided to try for the SAS. Being a natural survivor and blessed with strong nerves, he effortlessly passed Basic, Continuation and Cross-Training and was soon wearing the beret with winged dagger.

After another spell in Northern Ireland, practising counter-espionage in bandit country, he was posted to Oman, where he proved himself during the bloody, victorious advance on Shershitti. After that, he knew he'd remain an SAS trooper for as long as they let him.

Paddy didn't feel sentimental about being in the SAS – it was just a job he loved doing – and since he didn't have a family, let alone familial feelings, he withstood the mental stress of lengthy, silent vigils in OPs or scrapes by dwelling, as he was doing right here in East Falkland, on the excitements of his past and the ones he might have in the future.

Though in a cold, damp, coffin-shaped scrape, hidden under a false roof camouflaged with turf, hardly able to breathe, Paddy passed the day more easily than the others, feeling no more than boredom. He took his pride from his suffering.

By the third night they were passing through areas patrolled constantly by Argentinian troops, which meant that they had to be particularly careful and, even under cover of darkness, could advance only with great care. The urge to open fire was now stronger than ever – the humiliation of the Royal

Marines at Port Stanley still rankled – but their training stood them in good stead and, instead of firing, they simply laid low again and took note of the troop movements, their numbers and weapons. Similar notes were taken on the movements, now more frequent, of Argentinian helicopters and aircraft.

Eventually, after three days and nights, just before dawn on the third night, they reached the high ground overlooking Port Stanley and located the ridge chosen for the OP.

'This is it,' Ricketts said with confidence, checking his map against the actual location. 'Let's dig in, lads.'

Still protected by moonlit darkness, using spades and pickaxes while Danny stood guard, they quickly, expertly, constructed a rectangular OP, employing the standard techniques that had recently been used by Grenville in South Georgia. So high and exposed was the ridge that there was little natural cover from the elements, enemy patrols or aircraft. For this reason they camouflaged the OP with a roof of turf over the usual supporting material.

If nothing else, this would hide them from the thermal imagers of Argentinian helicopters. Whether or not it would hide them from enemy foot patrols was, as Ricketts knew from past experience, questionable.

Under normal circumstances, from the OP position, their signaller, Paddy, would have established communications with the SAS base, entertainingly located in the ladies' toilet aboard the *Resource*. However, because it was feared that they might be located by the Argentinians through the pick-up of their radio signals, Major Parkinson had ordered them to maintain radio silence until just before returning to the fleet. Therefore, for the next three days, the information already gathered, as well as the fresh intelligence picked up from the OP and by dangerous foot recces down the hill, to near the Argentinian positions in Port Stanley, was not transmitted, but kept in a file that would be destroyed should the enemy close in on them.

The OP had only one narrow aperture, but it offered a good view of Stanley airport and the Argentinian positions in the surrounding hills. Valuable intelligence was gathered daily with the use of black-painted, camouflaged binoculars, telescopes and night-vision aids. Visual information was usually photographed and the details overdrawn on maps and aerial photos taken by previous aircraft recces. Other information was entered in the logbook as it came up.

Throughout the three days, Argentinian helicopters made reconnaissance sweeps over the
hillside. Occasionally foot patrols could be seen
on the lower slopes leading down to Port Stanley
and the airport. This made foot recces more
dangerous for Ricketts and his men, but they
made them nevertheless, usually under cover of
darkness, when they were guided to the enemy
positions by the glow of their fires or the lights
shining inside occupied buildings.

Sometimes Argentinian soldiers marched past,
only a few feet away from where the SAS recce
team was lying, pressed tight to the earth.

To just lie there, doing nothing, was not only
frustrating, but required unusually cool nerves.
Yet all of them preferred the danger to the boredom of spending all day and night in the OP,
where the light was too dim even for reading
(notes were entered in the logbook by torchlight)
and the only distraction was listening to the BBC
World Service through muffled headphones. This
at least kept them abreast of political and military
developments regarding the Falklands.

The situation, they learned, was reaching crisis
point. This was proven by the fact that Port
Stanley's airport was now being bombed from the
air and bombarded from sea every night, offering

the men in the OP a tremendous, fiery spectacle that illuminated the dark port while blotting out the stars with billowing black smoke.

Always, when this happened, the Argentinian helicopters took off from the erupting airport, crossing directly over the OP as they fled inland. Just as often, when they returned, some of them would be missing, having been shot down by the fleet's Harrier jets after being located by other SAS OPs, located much further away from the Argentinian positions and so not under radio restrictions.

The nightly bombings and bombardments became an enjoyable form of distraction for the men in the OP.

After gathering all the information he could reasonably expect to find, Ricketts took a chance and radioed it back to base, with a request that the team be picked up as soon as possible. Confirmation came that the helicopter was on its way and would be there in approximately forty minutes.

'Right, men,' Ricketts said, 'let's pack up and leave. Danny, you take point as sentry while we dismantle and fill in the OP.'

'OK, boss,' the baby-faced trooper said, immediately picking up his M16, clambering out of the

OP, and slithering down the slope for about fifteen yards, to take up his position behind an outcrop of rock, overlooking the lights of the otherwise darkened port. Ricketts, Paddy and Andrew then packed up their kit, dismantled the OP and buried as much as possible beneath the earth, which they then flattened and covered with loose soil.

Fifteen minutes before the helo was due to descend for the pick-up, an Argentinian foot patrol made its way up the hill, the three men in triangular formation, weapons at the ready. It was obvious they had located the approximate area of the OP from the radio call made by Ricketts to the fleet.

The Argentinians investigated the dark, slightly moonlit ridge in a criss-crossing pattern, then spread out even farther as they advanced towards the summit – one, the scout, being too far ahead of the others for his own good.

Ricketts cursed softly and was about to tell his men to open fire – which might have exposed them to other enemy troops hidden lower down the slope – when Danny waved his right hand behind him in an up-and-down motion, signalling that Ricketts and the others should stay flat and remain out of sight. They obeyed his instruction just as the Argentinian scout stepped past Danny's position, missing him by inches, to advance straight up the hill towards Ricketts.

The other Argentinians were not even looking when Danny rose silently, a mere shadow against the skyline, and applied the silent killing technique by coming up behind his victim, covering his mouth with one hand and swiftly slashing his jugular vein with his Fairburn-Sykes commando knife. He held the body tightly while lowering it to the ground before it could go into spasm and start thrashing noisily.

Danny killed the man skilfully, with great stealth and speed, and was moving, crouched over, towards his next victim even before the first soldier was dead.

The second death occurred in darkness, completely hidden from view. There was just a brief thrashing sound – a falling body crushing bracken – then the last Argentinian, hearing the noise, looked around him in panic. His face was visible in the moonlight, eyes wide, searching frantically, but even as he started turning his rifle to fire, a white hand covered his mouth and jerked his head back, enabling a gleaming, moonlit blade to slit his throat.

The soldier's body shuddered convulsively as Danny's other hand slipped around it. His rifle fell from twitching fingers as he spasmed, staying upright, held tightly by his killer, then was lowered gently, almost tenderly, to the ground, to be rolled over and pressed face down into soft soil, which silenced his final, dying gurgle.

Eventually, after checking that the man was dead, Danny stood up and extended his right hand, waving it in towards his body, signalling: 'As you were.'

Ricketts and the others heaved a sigh of relief, then stood up to gather their kit together and await the helo's arrival.

Danny walked back up the slope, his rifle slung across his shoulders, wiping his bloody blade on a cloth and smiling dreamily at them.

'No problem,' he conveyed without speaking, simply raising his thumb in the air. Ricketts replied in kind.

The helo arrived on time, hardly visible in the dark sky, its presence only evident from the sound of its engine and spinning rotors, first a distant throbbing sound, then a drumming and whipping, and finally a roaring that decimated the silence. It descended quickly, hovering just above the ground, whipping up a minor hurricane of flying debris. Then it was ascending again even before the last of the men, Ricketts, had heaved his heavy kit aboard and clambered in after it.

'Piece of piss,' Andrew said.

9

'I've called this briefing,' Captain Grenville said in the ladies' toilet of the *Resource*, 'because we're going in on another urgent recce.'

Corporal Jock McGregor and troopers Taff Burgess and Gumboot Gillis glanced at one another with the air of men being offered a release from prison. They were also pleased to be given the chance to do something, now that the war with Argentina had truly begun.

The day after Ricketts and his patrol had been inserted on East Falkland, the British submarine HMS *Conqueror* had sunk the Argentinian heavy cruiser the *General Belgrano*. This had led to jubilation among the members of the fleet, but this was brutally extinguished when, two days later, an Exocet missile fired from an Argentinian Super Etendard warplane sank HMS *Sheffield*, resulting in many British dead and wounded.

During that time three British Harriers were also lost, one shot down, two colliding over the sea. The war with Argentina was well and truly engaged, making the frustrated members of the SAS itch to take part and make amends for their own recent disasters.

'The various recce patrols of East Falkland,' Captain Grenville continued, 'produced enough intelligence to enable us to launch a major offensive against the island as the first step on the road to Port Stanley. The intended landing beaches are at San Carlos Water, on the west coast of East Falkland, but before the landings can take place we have to destroy any Argentinian aircraft that are within range of the beaches. At the moment, all we know is that those aircraft are based on a grass strip near the only settlement on Pebble Island.'

'Our destination,' Jock said.

'Exactly.'

'Do we know anything else about the aircraft?' Gumboot asked, scratching the broken nose that lent a distorted appearance to his ferret-like face.

'Only that they include 1A-58 Pucara ground-attack planes built in Argentina for use against lightly armed forces. Each carries 20mm cannons, four 7.62mm machine-guns and bombs or rockets, all of which can be used when flying slowly, to strafe our ground troops.'

'How many?' Taff Burgess asked, rubbing his big belly and offering the other two his familiar, distant smile.

'That's what we have to find out.'

'Then we destroy them.'

'No. Then we report back here. Once we've brought the intelligence back, the green slime will decide the next course of action.'

'Shit,' Jock said, then coughed into his fist and glanced around him. It was difficult to breathe in the toilet because of the dense cigarette smoke, most of which came from the constantly burning fags of the radio operatives set up near the toilet booths. 'Hell of a place for our base,' Jock observed. 'Makes me feel right queer, boss.'

'Maybe that's because you *are* queer,' Gumboot responded.

'Yes, dear,' Taff said.

'Come on, men, cut the bullshit,' Captain Grenville said. 'We've no time to spare.'

'So what do we know about Pebble Island?' Jock asked sensibly.

'We believe there's a radar station on the island, although electronic checks have shown that if there is one, it's not being operated. However, they may just be maintaining radio silence until the right moment and we can't risk having our amphibious ships detected as they near Pebble Island, en route to San Carlos Water – so eyeball recces, rather than airborne or electronic surveillance, are required.'

'The good old-fashioned way,' Jock observed.

'Right, Corporal,' Captain Grenville said. 'Which is why we're going in by boat again, instead of by helo.'

'Suits me,' Taff Burgess said. 'When do we leave?'

'When you're kitted out, Trooper.'

'So let's go and do it.'

Leaving the cramped, smoky toilet, they made their way down through the creaking, throbbing bowels of the ship to the SAS requisition area. When they entered the hold filled with makeshift tables laden with all kinds of military clothing, including tropical and Arctic wear, and stacked with crates of weapons, radios and food supplies, they found Ricketts and his team handing back the equipment they had used for their recent OP overlooking Port Stanley. Ricketts was signing his name on a form while the others, some smoking, were waiting for him.

'Well, well,' Jock said with a wicked grin directed at Ricketts, Paddy, Danny and big Andrew, 'the Boy Scouts managed to find their way back after their day out.'

'So where are you lot off to?' Ricketts replied, handing the requisitions clerk the pen and paper, then turning to face the Boat Troop. 'Another Girl Guides' outing, is it, lads?'

'You'd know more about the Girl Guides than we would,' Gumboot said, 'since they're in the only age range you could manage – *if* you could manage it.'

'Another recce?' young Danny asked, baby-faced yet more serious than the others.

'Right,' Taff said with a distant smile.

'Come down to us for some advice, have you?' big Andrew asked, brown eyes bright in that handsome ebony face. 'You know we're dependable.'

'I'd be safer depending on a fucking Argie,' Paddy said. 'Advice from *you* lot? Don't come it, mate!'

'OK,' Captain Grenville said, 'that's enough of the bullshit. This is a confidential mission, Sergeant Ricketts, so get your men out of here.'

'Yes, boss,' Ricketts replied. He turned to the rest of Grenville's team. 'Don't take any notice of these lads. They're just trying to be helpful. Given the reputation of the Boat Troop, they figure you need it.' He turned away while the mocking comments flew thick and fast. 'Come on, lads, let's go. Let the girls do their business.'

Hoots of derision followed the laughing exit of the Mountain Troop, then, after quietening down his men, Captain Grenville requisitioned the weapons and equipment needed for the recce. These included waterproof clothing, special survival suits, life-jackets, a waterproof PRC 319 radio system, and SARBE rescue beacons.

While the men were putting on their waterproof clothing, Grenville phoned through to the docking bay, asking them to prepare two Klepper canoes for his four-man patrol. By the time he had put on his own waterproof gear, the men had received their packed, heavy bergens and were checking their weapons. When they were satisfied, Grenville led them out of the hold and even deeper into the bowels of the ship, until they arrived at the docking bay, which was open and flooded, with the canoes already placed in the water by the Naval ratings who worked here.

As it was nearly midnight, the interior of the docking bay, which resembled a vast hangar, was eerily lit by dimmed spotlights that could not be seen by enemy aircraft, but made the open stern, as well as the sea beyond it, seem even darker and more mysterious than it was. Large Landing Craft, Vehicle Personnel, or LCVPs, were anchored in the water between the three great steel walls, with the smaller Rigid Raiders, five metres long and with fibre-glass hulls, suspended from cranes directly above them. Inflatable Geminis, now all deflated, hung from the walls.

'They look like giant johnnies', Jock observed, 'but they'd be too small for me.'

Taff chuckled.

'Quiet, troopers,' Grenville said, picking up his bergen onto his shoulders, raising his waterproof cape over his head and gazing down at the Klepper canoe just below him. 'Gumboot, you come with me. You two,' he said to Jock and Taff, 'can share the other canoe. OK, let's move it.'

Luckily, the sea was calm, enabling them to load their bergens and weapons into the prow and rear areas of the canoes, cover the hull with a waterproof covering and insert themselves into the two holes in the covering. Once seated, one man behind the other, they tightened the waterproof covering around their waists, picked up their oars and told the Naval ratings to untie the ropes and push them away from the dock. When the ratings had done so, setting them free in the water, they rowed the canoes out of the docking bay and into the dark, open sea.

Normally, the patrol would have cross-decked to a submarine and let it take them close to the shore, but in the absence of a suitable submarine, the *Resource* had sailed under radio silence close enough to the shore for Pebble Island to be visible to the naked eye. What the men in the canoes now saw was a strip of featureless, dark land with few visible hills.

Taking his bearings from the moon and stars, which that night were clearly visible, Grenville led the second canoe towards the approximate area of the chosen LZ, confident that when he drew closer to the shore, he would be able to arrive at the exact location by using the landmarks he had memorized from intelligence briefings. As the ship had managed to get to within a couple of miles of the shore, the canoes were soon in shallow water, with the beach clearly visible, striped by shadow and moonlight, and leading gently up to low hills on which patches of ice gleamed blue and white.

Still paddling with the others, Grenville scanned

the length of the shore for camp-fires or other signs of the enemy presence. So far there was nothing. After bending his right arm, hand raised to indicate 'halt', he again took his bearings, this time with a combination of compass reading and a visual check of the fall of land. Now knowing exactly where the LZ was located, he took the time to jot down useful notes of the tides (which he had observed during the journey), beach gradients that would be suitable for amphibious landings and general topographical details that would help in selecting the best areas for the advance by foot soldiers. This done, he pocketed his pen and notebook, then gently waved his outstretched hand up and down, practically touching the water's surface, to indicate that the other canoe should follow him.

Starting to row again, with Gumboot expertly doing the same behind him, he was soon gliding through shallow water and coming up on the beach. At his signal, Gumboot and the others stopped rowing, anchored the canoes, removed the protective waterproofing from the top of the hull, then carefully clambered out and splashed down into the water. After offloading their kit and weapons, which they carried bit by bit to the shore, they pulled the canoes in, carried them carefully across the beach to ensure that they would not be damaged, stored them under sparse, overhanging foliage, then constructed chicken-wire covers for them. These were then camouflaged with turf and more local foliage.

Finally, with the canoes safely hidden, they strapped the overloaded bergens onto their backs and, at another silent signal from Captain Grenville, hurried off the exposed beach and began the march up the gentle, moonlit slopes of wind-blown grass towards where the Argentinian airstrip was located. They had not spoken a word since leaving the ship forty minutes ago.

The march took them over the low hills and back down again, then along a narrow waist of land with the sea on each side, open and exposed, without natural cover anywhere. This eventually led them to the estimated mile-and-a-quarter field where the aircraft, visible in moonlight, were dispersed.

Viewing them through binoculars, from behind a hedgerow on a slight rise about two miles from the grass airfield, Grenville was able to see the heavily armed Argentinian troops guarding them. Swinging the binoculars in both directions, to view the sea on both sides of the long, narrow strip, he saw the camp-fires of many other enemy positions, placed there as protection against attacks from the sea. According to the green slime, an estimated one hundred Argentinian troops were surrounding the airfield.

'Let's dig in here,' Grenville said, speaking for the first time since leaving the ship. 'We'll recce the whole area as quickly as we can, then get the hell out. They want us back with the fleet as soon as possible, so let's waste no time. Jock, you stick with the radio and be guard.'

'Aye, aye,' Jock said, then moved forward to a more advantageous viewpoint, offering the protection of bushes from where he could see the still darkened airstrip, as well as all around him.

'We'll only be here a short time,' Grenville said. 'So make the OP a star shape.'

'Right, boss,' Taff said, unstrapping his bergen, lowering it to the ground, then opening it, as Gumboot was also doing, to withdraw his pickaxe and spade for the digging.

The star-shaped OP serves the same function as the rectangular, but is smaller and easier to construct. It is shaped like a cross with four arms of equal length: one for the sentry, one for the observer, one as a personal admin, or short-term rest bay, the last as a proper rest bay for a longer, more comfortable sleep in a sleeping bag. Covered, like the rectangular OP, in ponchos, turf and other available materials, such as local brush or shrubbery, it has an open drainage well in the middle, into which excess water, such as rain, will run, and it also contains a kit-well. Giving good all-round visibility, it is excellent as a short-term OP that can be quickly constructed and just as quickly filled in and disguised, as if it had never been.

With the OP constructed, Grenville took the sentry arm, which overlooked the grassy strip and airfield. Studying it through his binoculars as the sun came up, he was able to count eleven Pucaras. As the sun rose higher in the sky, he saw that the Argentinian troops were indeed spread right around the airfield and along the narrow strip of land with the sea on both sides. He also noticed, with a slight shock, that the ground on which the planes were parked was on the top of another rise that put it on the same level as the OP.

'Damn!' Grenville whispered.

'What's that, boss?' Jock asked from the personal admin rest bay.

'I thought we were on a rise, but the slope rises again to put the airstrip on the same level as the OP. That's going to make it damned difficult to get away from here without our movements being noticed by the Argies, even in darkness. We're going to be silhouetted by the sky.'

Jock sat up and expertly scanned the area. 'Aye, you're right there. On the other hand . . .' His eyes moved left and right, then settled on the right. He jabbed his index finger in that direction. 'There's a slight depression over there, running back towards the sea in the general direction of the LZ. We'll have to take our chances and crawl along that.'

Grenville studied the depression with some care. 'Right,' he said eventually. 'Let's do that. We don't have much choice. We'll take off when darkness falls. In the meantime, let's take note of as much as possible without leaving the OP.'

Jock studied the airstrip and both sides of the strip through his own binoculars. 'Those sentries don't look particularly alert to me,' he said with a slight trace of contempt. 'I reckon you could go for a Sunday walk and they wouldn't even notice.'

'I reckon you'd get your balls shot off, so don't try it, Corporal.'

'Aye, aye, boss, I hear you.'

As the day progressed it became increasingly evident that the Argentinian sentries were indeed not very alert and certainly not expecting to find British soldiers spying from the edge of their well-guarded, wind-blown airstrip. And yet it was also clear that any attempt to move out of the OP would result in being spotted immediately. Grenville and his men therefore settled in for a long, cramped, tedious watch, taking turns in the sentry arm and passing on to the others anything they had seen that might be of the slightest interest.

Of most interest was the fact that the enemy sentries were obviously not expecting a British assault in the immediate future – a mistaken notion that had made them lax – and that their aircraft, the eleven Pucaras, were not being used and probably would not be until the actual assault began. It would certainly therefore be wise to put them out of action before D-Day.

While the Argentinian troops moved constantly up and down both sides of the strip throughout the day, sometimes on foot, more often in jeeps and trucks, they never ventured away from the airstrip, nor came in the direction of the OP. By the time the sun had started sinking, Grenville knew all there was to know about the airstrip and its defences.

'Time to move out,' he said.

The star-shaped OP was demolished and filled in under the cover of darkness, though that in itself was dangerous enough. Mission completed, they packed everything back into their bergens, checked their weapons, took one last look at the airstrip, where lights were winking on here and there, then ran, crouched low, to the slight depression that snaked around the top of the hill and led back towards the sea. Unfortunately, it did so in a way that took them dangerously close to the Argentinian sentries, which is why, even before they reached the depression, they had to drop onto their bellies and virtually crawl to it.

'Shit!' Taff exclaimed in a whisper.

'What?' Grenville enquired.

'My bergen's jutting over the top of the depression.'

'So's mine,' Gumboot whispered.

They stared at one another, eyes gleaming in descending darkness, then Grenville said, 'We don't have a choice. We'll have to take the bergens off and leave them here.'

'If they're found,' Jock pointed out, 'the Argies will know we've been here and guess that the British assault is imminent.'

'I know,' Grenville replied, 'but we still don't have a choice. It's either that or be seen for sure.

We've been here all day and the Argies haven't come near this area, so let's just pray that they won't for the next few days. Come on, chaps, let's dump them.'

The four of them struggled out of their bergens, which wasn't easy to do without sitting up, but eventually, when they had been discarded, they moved off again, holding their M16s out ahead of them as they wriggled on their bellies along the depression, practically chewing the soil.

This agonizingly slow, physically draining form of movement had to be continued for approximately half a mile, which took them a torturous three hours to cover. By the time they were out of sight of the Argentinians, they were sweating even in the freezing cold; they were also covered in dirt and breathing harshly. Nevertheless, now out of sight of the enemy, they climbed to their feet and began the rest of their six-mile march back to the beach.

Still blessed by darkness, they uncovered the Klepper canoes, carried them back to the water, anchored and loaded them, clambered in, pulled the anchors in and rowed themselves back out to sea. When they were out a reasonable distance, seeing nothing but the stars sharply cut off by the sea's black horizon, Jock used the radio for the first time, informing the *Resource* that they were on their way back and giving their location. In return, he was informed that the ship was coming in as close to the shore as possible to pick them up. He was to signal the ship with his Morse-code lamp as soon as he saw it.

About forty minutes later, when they were rowing in a black sea reflecting the star-bright sky, they glided into a patch of dense fog. A few minutes later the *Resource* came into view, materializing eerily out of the fog-filled darkness, towering over them as an immense rectangle on which lights glowed dimly.

Jock picked up his signalling lamp and sent a message in Morse code, identifying the two Kleppers, giving the name of their occupants and asking for permission to row around the ship and enter the docking bay. Permission was received by another light flashing in Morse code. It flashed on and off high above them, then signalled 'Over and out' and blinked off, leaving only the darkness.

With his right hand Jock signalled 'Follow me', then he and Grenville started rowing, leading Taff and Gumboot around the ghostly ship, illuminated dimly by the lights that shone high above them.

In the darkness, beyond the fog, the great

ship creaked and groaned as if alive. The sea, though relatively calm, beat and splashed relentless against its hull, making a dull drumming sound.

Eventually the stern of the ship came into view, first as a mere sliver of light on the black water, then as a vertical rectangle of light in which tiny, silhouetted figures moved back and forth, finally as a towering square of light that appeared to be burning out of three immense walls of steel – actually the inside of the ship's hull – from which hung deflated Geminis. Below the inflatables were suspended Rigid Raiders and, in the water between the steel catwalks, anchored LCVPs.

As the two canoes drifted into the docking bay someone cried out, 'Welcome home!'

The four men in the canoes gave the thumbs-up, grinning like Cheshire cats.

10

'The date for the assault on Pebble Beach,'
Major Parkinson informed captains Hailsham
and Grenville on the deck of the Fleet flagship HMS *Hermes* shortly after the Squadron
had been cross-decked by helicopter from the
Resource, 'has been brought forward from 21
to 15 May.'

'Why?' Hailsham asked, since this would dras-
tically reduce the time his Mountain Troop had
for briefing and preparation. 'That only leaves
us two days.'

Major Parkinson sighed. 'I know. The problem
is that the three Sea King helos required for the
insertion are only available for ten hours each
day. As they have to be serviced, and since
the nights of the sixteenth and nineteenth are
scheduled for the re-supply and debriefing of
recce patrols, any landing on Pebble Island will

have to be made before the sixteenth. The raid has therefore been rescheduled to the early hours of the fifteenth. We'll just have to make do.'

Shading his eyes with one hand to protect them from the wind and spray, Parkinson was forced to squint as he studied the many activities taking place on the enormous deck of the ship. Despite the aircraft-carrier's size, the *Hermes* was presently steaming into strong headwinds that made her roll heavily in the surging waves. Because her secondary role of anti-submarine helicopter carrier had added many helos to her complement of Harrier jets, she had a flight deck angled at 6.5 degrees with a 7-degree, gleaming white ski-jump ramp that appeared, from where Parkinson was standing, to soar all the way up to the stormy sky. The immense deck, which was rising and falling hypnotically against a backdrop of stormy sea, was littered with Sea Harrier jets. Sea King helicopters, with folded blades, were parked forward, near piles of strapped-down 1000lb cluster bombs. Four LCVP landing-craft were slung in davits. The jackstay rigs and derricks were a brilliant, blinding yellow against the off-white ship and surrounding grey sea.

With 1027 ratings and 143 officers, the *Hermes* was like a floating Air Force base, always busy, noisy, and wind-blown, with huge waves – though the sea seemed impossibly far below – often smashing noisily against the hull, hurling spray over the deck and soaking the busy ratings. Major Parkinson, not easily impressed, was very impressed.

'There's another small problem,' he said quietly.

'Please *do* tell me, boss,' Captain Hailsham enthused sarcastically.

'These headwinds have prevented the helos being prepared in advance, which is going to cause another slight delay. The storm is expected to abate by this afternoon, but because we'll be late in loading the helos, our time to complete the mission will be reduced from 90 minutes to 30.'

'With all due respect, boss, that's asking an awful lot from our lads.'

Parkinson sighed again. 'I know, but I'm sure they can manage. Get in, do the job, and get out. It's a hit-and-run mission. At least we're no longer expected to eliminate the Argentinian ground crews and the rest of the island's garrison, as well as destroying the planes. As our time has been reduced from 90 minutes to 30, the attack has been limited to destroying the aircraft and ensuring that our helos are back aboard the *Hermes* before daylight. This in turn will ensure that she and her escorts will be well to the east of the islands before the Argentinian Air Force can attack them, if they decide to do so.'

'Let's make sure we hit every plane on the ground,' Captain Hailsham said. 'Every damned one of them.'

'I still say we insert by boat,' Captain Grenville offered, sounding aggrieved.

'No,' Parkinson replied. 'We don't have the time. This is a surprise attack, so we have to insert by helo. Sorry, Larry, but you're out of this one. You'll be back here acting as base, in constant radio contact. You'll get us in and out.'

Hailsham raised his eyebrows at Grenville and gave a broad, mocking grin. 'Ah, well,' he said. 'A man's got to do what a man's got to do. Shall we adjourn to the briefing room?'

'Yes,' Parkinson said. 'The Squadron's already been gathered together there. They're all primed and waiting.'

'Then let's talk to them, boss.'

After another glance at the immense, swaying deck and the stormy sea beyond, Parkinson turned away and slipped through the nearest hatchway, leading the other two into the depths of the ship, down steel ladders, through more hatchways, along creaking corridors, past cabins and lockers and the operational area, to the hold containing the ship's large briefing room. The members of the Mountain Troop, together with the SBS members who had just made the recce, were sitting in chairs in front of the big blackboard, now covered in maps of Pebble Island.

The babble of conversation died away when Parkinson entered the room with his two officers and took his place on the small, raised platform in front of the maps. He picked up a pointer and tapped the map behind him, letting the pointer rest on Pebble Beach.

'There it is, gentlemen – our LZ. The beach on Pebble Island. That island is the stepping-stone to San Carlos Water, which is, of course, the back door to Port Stanley. Our job is to ensure the safety of the forthcoming landings by putting all the Argentinian aircraft on Pebble Island out of business. How does that grab you?'

A cheer went up from the assembled men, only dying away when Parkinson waved them into silence.

'What about the Argies?' Ricketts asked.

'Right,' Danny said, looking and sounding, as always, like a choirboy. 'Do we mop 'em up?'

'No,' Parkinson said. 'We no longer have time for that. We've had an hour lopped off our schedule, which only leaves 30 minutes for the actual raid on the airstrip. Our job, therefore, is to ensure that all their aircraft are immobilized in that time – then we get the hell out. We're not interested in taking prisoners or a high body-count. Our sole interest has to be the aircraft.'

'How many?' Ricketts asked.

'Eleven Pucaras.'

Big Andrew gave a low whistle. 'That's some job to do in thirty minutes, boss.'

'You don't think you can manage it?'

'Didn't say that, boss. Merely observing that the time is pretty limited for that number of targets.'

'No argument, Trooper.'

'Who does what?' Jock McGregor asked.

'The Mountain Troop, led by myself and Captain Hailsham, will attack the planes, using LAW 66mm one-shot anti-tank rockets and small-arms fire. This will be done under cover of the Squadron mortars, to be handled by the Boat Troop, as well as a barrage from the fleet's big guns. We'll be guided from the LZ to the target by the members of the Boat Troop who performed the original recce . . .'

'The Girl Guides!' Paddy Clarke cried out, prompting an outburst of laughter and applause.

'At least we know our way around,' Gumboot retaliated with a grin. 'We don't get lost and return like a bunch of snowmen. We don't melt in the heat.'

This time it was the members of the Boat Troop who laughed and cheered while the Mountain Troop hurled good-natured insults.

'OK! OK!' Captain Hailsham said, raising his hand. 'That's enough of the bullshit. Quieten down now.'

Major Parkinson waited until the noise had abated, then continued: 'Let me repeat: the Boat Troop will lead us to the target, then man the mortars. A second troop will seal off the approaches to the airstrip, with a third troop held in reserve. When the planes are all hit, we retreat, still being covered by the mortars and the guns of the fleet. We don't detour en route back to the beach – no unnecessary engagements with the Argies, no laying of booby traps. We just retreat to the beach and get lifted off. Is that understood?'

There followed much nodding and shrugging, disgusted looks and the odd, disappointed, 'Yeah, yeah'.

'So,' Parkinson said, 'any questions?'

'When's the insertion?' big Andrew asked.

'The day after tomorrow. Midnight.'

'And the full briefing?'

'Tomorrow. You'll be at it all day. Intelligence from the green slime, kitted out by the REMFs, weapons-checking and practice all afternoon, a full inspection that evening. This procedure will be repeated the following day, with a final briefing just before insertion. You'll be kept busy, chaps.'

This produced groans, the shaking of heads and much rolling of eyeballs.

'Right, lads, class dismissed.'

The men pushed their chairs back and filed out of the briefing room, leaving Parkinson, Hailsham and Grenville alone by the black-board.

A lot of bullshit was flying in the hold of the ship, where the SAS troopers were preparing for the raid by urinating, defecating, having a shower, shaving, resting on their cramped steel bunks, one practically on top of the other, writing last-minute letters – or, in Andrew's case, some fine lines of poetry – smoking, drinking – though only non-alcoholic beverages were permitted before a raid – arranging their equipment in their bergens and checking their weapons. The hold was gloomy and sweltering, filled with sweat and the stench of farts, but this was the time they most enjoyed, so nobody cared – even though they certainly noticed the farting and used it for bullshit.

'Christ, that stench is goin' to kill me!' Paddy said. 'Who the hell farted?'

'I's innocent, Massa Abe,' Andrew cried out melodramatically, doing his plantation-nigger act, rolling his brown eyes and flashing his teeth. 'Lord have mercy upon me!'

'I'd recognize that stench anywhere,' Gumboot said, 'and it doesn't come out of a white man's arse. Own up, poet – you did it.'

'Leave him alone,' Taff said, smiling dreamily into his bergen, trying to work out what to put where. 'Being a poor black, he gets enough flak in Civvy Street. We don't want him breaking down in tears here because we've been cruel to him.'

'That's what I like to hear,' Andrew said. 'A little bit of compassion. Especially when it comes from the bastard who started this whole filthy conversation. Own up, Taff! Only a Welshman smells like that, so no point in denying it.'

'My arse isn't black, Trooper.'

'I've never seen mine,' countered Andrew. 'If you've managed to get a look at your own, I'd like to know when and how come. In your salty youth, was it?'

'Now that's wicked,' Jock said. 'That's stickin' it to him where it hurts. I'd be buggered before I'd wear that suggestion. So how *did* you see it, Taff?'

'Why are you all picking on me?'

'Because you fart like a camel.'

'You do that every time you open your mouth, Jock, so don't land on me. In fact, it was probably little baby-faced Danny Boy, now pretending he's deaf.'

Danny didn't respond. He just blushed and checked his weapons, concentrating fiercely on the job and looking at no one.

'Don't pick on that boy,' Jock said, trying to untangle his webbing, ammunition belts resting on his crossed legs, his kit littering his bunk. 'Innocence is bliss. Baby Face is as clean as his dagger when it slits a man's throat. His fart must smell like perfume.'

'I agree,' Gumboot said. 'Let's not upset Danny Boy. When it comes to the crunch tomorrow, when the heat's on, he's the one we'll depend on. He has nerves of steel, that kid.'

'And a rod of iron,' Taff said.

'Ah, jealousy!' Andrew said. 'I only know that when push comes to shove, it's the kid who's right in there.'

'Thanks, Andrew,' Danny said, checking his weapons, keeping his eyes down, speaking as softly as a girl. 'I don't want any bullshit from these bastards. I just want to take out some Argies and show them who's boss.'

'Quite right, too,' Andrew agreed. 'I like a man who knows his own mind. It's nice to know you'll be the boss in your own home when you and Darlene get married.'

'When's that, then?' Paddy enquired.

'Haven't decided yet,' Danny said. 'We were just about to work something out when the Argies gave aggro.'

'Most inconvenient,' Andrew said.

'Oh, I dunno,' Gumboot put in. 'I think Danny might be happier fighting Argies than banging his missus.'

'She's not his missus yet, Gumboot. They're only engaged at this point. And naturally you'd be cynical about that, given the state of *your* marriage.'

'His missus left him for a farmer,' Paddy explained helpfully to Danny. 'Gumboot won't tell us why and we're not about to pry, but we figure it's that problem between his legs. It's not a problem you'll have, kid.'

'Go fuck yourself,' Gumboot said.

'I hear poetry!' Andrew cried. 'Paddy Clarke has just spoken. Won't tell us why and we're not about to pry. I have serious competition in the ranks. Irish genius is rampant!'

'We're a talented race.'

'He's a Scouse, not an Irishman.'

'I'm whatever you farts want me to be, because I'll need you tomorrow.'

'What you need you may not get.'

'I stick my neck out for no one.'

'At least it's a proper assault at last and not another OP.' Taff finished packing his bergen and hung it from his bunk, then picked up his short M203 grenade-launcher to check that it fitted into the clip beneath his M16 rifle. It seemed to work all right. 'I'm fed up sitting in mud, rain and piss in a hole in the ground. I want out and about again.'

'So do I,' Danny said, checking his weapons, thinking of Darlene, secretly shocked that it was hard to visualize her when he had work to do. 'I want to shoot me some Argies.'

'You're like my own son,' Gumboot said. 'I

mean the son I might have had. Judging by my missus he'd have been a lot like you – an innocent, sweet-faced little psychopath with a cutting edge to him. My fucking missus is barmy.'

'I'm just a soldier,' Danny said. 'I take pride in my work. I mean, there's nothin' personal in it at all – it's just a job to be done.'

'Then do it tomorrow, Danny. Get in there and shoot some Argies. This time we're going in for the jackpot and a nice bit of aggro. I'm sure you'll be pleased, kid.'

Danny was holding an L1A1 self-loading rifle, inspecting the magazine release catch, slamming the magazine in, ensuring that the Trilux sight clipped on properly, then checking the foresight. Satisfied, he put the rifle down and pulled out his commando knife, turning it slowly before his eyes to let the dim light flash off it. 'Yeah,' he said, drawling like an American or a rock star, blissed out, distracted, 'I guess you're right there.'

'That's no bullshit,' Andrew said.

Parkinson studied the empty chairs in the briefing room, trying to recall all the faces of his troopers, filled with pride at their courage, proud to be their commander, but also concerned at how much they were being asked to do in such a short time.

'Thirty minutes,' he said eventually, almost whispering, really talking to himself. 'It's not too long at all.'

'No,' Hailsham agreed, 'it's not . . . But perhaps it'll work to our advantage. In and out while the Argies are still blinking, wondering what the hell's happening.'

'Let's hope so,' Grenville said.

The three officers smiled at one another, then left the briefing room, going their separate ways at the next hatchway, each with his own job to do.

11

At 30 minutes before midnight on the night of 15 May, HMS *Hermes* was sailing under radio silence through calm, moonlit waters.

Not so calm was the immense flight deck, where, under brilliant spotlights, three Sea King helicopters were being prepared by Naval ratings to carry the many SAS troops milling about them. After two days of briefing by the green slime, weapons training on the open deck and repeated inspections of their weapons and equipment, the men were raring to go.

Grouped around the helos, they were surrounded by a vast array of weapons, including L1A1 self-loading rifles, or SLRs; L7A2 7.62mm general-purpose machine-guns, or GPMGs; M72 light anti-tank weapons, or LAWs; M16 and M203 grenade-launchers with cartridge-launched grenades; L16 ML 81mm mortars with calibrated

dial sights; white-phosphorus, smoke and fragmentation hand-grenades; and even the beloved
Browning 9mm high-power handguns.

As the plan was to get in and out quickly,
the bergens did not have to carry rucksacks
and sleeping bags, but some still weighed up
to 140lb because of the additional burdens of
heavy weaponry, including the mortars, extra
200-round belts for the GPMGs, radio systems,
batteries, binoculars, emergency rations and personal first-aid kits.

The heaviest equipment was being packed in
net-covered pallets by the Navy's flight-deck parties for transportation as underslung loads on
the helos. But the rest of it had to be carried by
the Troop in their bergens, which is why, combined with their bulky Gore-tex weatherproof
battle jackets, the men looked bowed down and
unwieldy.

Wearing ear protectors to combat the incessant
noise, or headsets for communications, the Royal
Naval Squadron ground crew and flight-deck
parties – all with their ranks and names on
a patch on their back for easy recognition –
worked ceaselessly at checking and loading the
helicopters. The Sea Harrier pilots – relatively
slim and dashing in their G-suits and thermal

liners, but with 9mm Browning automatic pistols on their hips – looked on, grinning widely, mixing encouragement with friendly banter.

The noise was atrocious. Even as the helicopters roared into life, with their rotor blades spinning and whipping up the air, some of the Sea Harriers lined along the edge of the deck were also revving up to make their way cautiously to the angled flight deck on the bow of the ship. Ignoring the planes, some of the SAS troops were running last-minute checks on their weapons by firing them off the edge of the flight deck at the stately white-capped waves. At the same time the bright-yellow jackstay rigs were moving equipment across the forward deck, before it was cross-decked to another ship later that day. Last but not least was the bawling of many men, trying to communicate with one another above the combined roaring, whining, screeching and clanging – not forgetting the moaning wind and the ceaseless bass rumbling of the sea as it hammered the ship's hull.

'Move it!' Major Parkinson yelled, scanning the sky beyond his helo and seeing a pale moon and myriad stars in the vast night sky. 'Let's do it! *Go!*'

As Ricketts was urging his men into the Sea Kings, one of the Sea Harriers roared into life, belching flames and smoke, then moved along the deck, raced up the angled flight deck and soared into the sky. Ricketts felt the blast from the take-off, as well as a wave of heat, even as his helo roared even louder and its spinning rotors, increasing their speed, created a minor hurricane that threatened to sweep him off his feet.

After glancing at the sea far below the helipad, Ricketts followed Paddy Clarke into the helo, moved along the cramped, vibrating interior, and strapped himself in between big Andrew and Danny. He was adjusting his belt when another Sea Harrier took off with a mighty roar that seemed to fill the already noisy interior of the helo, before fading away far out to sea.

As Ricketts was last in, the RAF Sergeant Air Loadmaster in charge of the hold, wearing an olive-green flying suit, zip-up boots and a headset for communication with the crew and ground crew, slammed and locked the door. After saying something into the mouthpiece of his headset, he disappeared behind the pallets stacked up along the front of the SAS Troop. A minute later, with much shaking and roaring, the helo lifted off the helipad, swayed from side to side, ascended vertically, hovered for a moment, then headed for the shore.

Glancing over his shoulder, through the window behind him, Ricketts saw the aircraft-carrier far below, cutting through the grey sea, its immense deck decorated with white-painted guide lines for the aircraft, the ski-jump ramp curving gracefully over the bow, the yellow jack-stays a startling contrast in colour even from this great height. The second Sea King was ascending just below, coming closer, and the third was rising off the helipad on the carrier's deck to follow the second. It was a sight worth seeing.

'How's it going, troopers?' he asked. 'No pissing in the pants? No diarrhoea?'

'Lots of uncomfortable smells down here, boss, but all of them are coming from the Boat Troop.'

When the laughter died away, Gumboot replied: 'The only diarrhoea down here, Trooper Winston, is the bullshit coming out of your mouth. It flows fast and free.'

Andrew yelped with pleasure, his teeth gleaming white. 'Oh, man, we got a gilded tongue there. These Girl Guides are so fast.'

'Fast and efficient. Competent and cool. You want poetry, Mr Poet, there it is. You can always call on the Boat Troop.'

'They always come when we call,' Paddy said deadpan.

'They come at the very sight of us,' Andrew added. 'They're so desperate, the poor dears.'

'Glad you're all still awake,' Ricketts said. 'I like my Girl Guides and Boy Scouts to be alert, even if just with bullshit. It keeps my pulse beating at a normal rate – but that's enough for now, children. Keep the lid on it.'

'Yes, boss, we hear you.'

The banter, which was competitive, was also good-humoured, relied on not only to pass the time during the flight, but to ease the tension felt by even the most courageous, experienced troopers before going into battle.

Ricketts had known a similar kind of ban-ter when on the North Sea oil rigs, where the constant danger and daily isolation had created the same kind of camaraderie. It was exactly what held the SAS together and made it such an effective fighting unit. Ricketts liked being part of it. Married though he was, good father that he was, he now knew he could never live a normal life outside the Regiment. For him, it all began and ended here, no matter what the danger.

'Keep your arses on your seats,' Gumboot said thirty minutes later. 'Here comes the Navy!'

'Actually, I'm RAF,' the Sergeant Air Load-master replied with an easy grin, returning to take his place by the exit door, 'and we're the guys that always get the ladies – we don't need you toy soldiers. Now unhitch yourselves and stand up, boyos. We're coming in for the landing.'

The repartee stopped immediately as the men concentrated on the job in hand, first unclipping their safety belts, then standing upright with a noisy jangling of weapons and turning into line, ready to leap out one by one when ordered to do so. The Loadmaster opened the door when the helo was still descending, letting the air rush in and howl through the hold, beating and tugging furiously at the men and their colliding weapons. Ricketts saw the sky outside, a stretch of darkness filled with stars, then a darker, tilting length of coastline as the helo changed its direction, heading for the LZ.

'Ten, nine, eight, seven,' the Loadmaster called, counting down. 'Three, two, one, zero . . . Go!'

The troopers jumped out one by one as the helo hovered in the air, swaying dangerously from side to side, mere feet off the ground. The first men down formed a protective ring around the helo, their weapons at the ready, while others released the underslung loads containing the heavy equipment. The helos remained in the air, creating a storm directly below, with sand and shrubbery spinning wildly, but the troopers fought against the swirling wind to spread out even farther.

When the men were all on the ground, either spreading out in a defensive circle or opening the underslung loads, the helos rose vertically, hovered briefly, in salute, then flew back towards the Fleet, leaving the LZ in a calmer state and letting the men get to work.

The helos had touched down on an LZ marked by the Boat Troop and located approximately six miles from the airstrip. Once the pallets had been broken open and the equipment dispersed, Major Parkinson quietly briefed the other officers, then divided the Squadron into three separate groups.

'Group One will seal off all approaches to the airstrip,' Parkinson explained, 'to ensure that the Argies can't get in *or* out. Group Two, led by myself, will blow up the Argentinian aircraft. The third group – and I know you won't like this – will be held in reserve.'

When the men in Group Three started beefing, Parkinson silenced them with a wave of his hand.

'Sorry, men, but that's the way it has to be.

I just can't commit all of you. Now where are the men who went on the original recce?' Jock, Gumboot and Taff raised their hands. 'Right,' Parkinson said. 'It's up to you three to lead us off the beach and guide us to the airstrip, stopping at the previously laid base-plate to set up the mortar. You do *remember* the route?'

'Yes, boss,' Jock said.

'And you *did* lay down a base-plate for the mortar en route back to the LZ?'

'That's A1 as well, boss.'

'OK, then, let's move out.'

This time, when they embarked on their long march, there were no jokes about Girl Guides.

In fact, the bright moonlight made most of them feel vulnerable as they hiked across four miles of desolate, exposed moorland to the site chosen by the Boat Patrol for the mortar base-plate, approximately two and half miles from the airstrip. Each member of the squadron was carrying two bombs for the mortar, which they left with the selected mortar crew – Gumboot and Taff – by the steel base-plate earlier laid down by them in this clearing, within a handily protective circle of piled rocks.

'Now I believe in miracles,' Paddy said. 'They actually remembered to lay it down.'

'Fucking right, we did,' Jock said. 'When we do a job, we do it properly. You need lessons? Just ask.'

'OK, troopers,' Ricketts said. 'That's enough of the mutual admiration. Now go about your business.'

'Good as done,' Gumboot said, then he and Taff, observed thoughtfully by Major Parkinson and Ricketts, set up the L16 ML 81mm mortar, which would be fired indirectly at a target identified by a forward observer placed with the assault group at the airstrip and using a PRC 319 radio system for communication with the mortar crew.

As the mortar had a range of three miles, it was well within range of the target airstrip, approximately two and a half miles distant. The forward observer would be Corporal Clarke.

'Right, boss,' Gumboot said, sitting back on his haunches and admiring the mortar now fixed to its base-plate. 'We're all set to go.'

'Good,' Parkinson replied. 'We'll be in contact as soon as we reach the airstrip. Tune that radio, Trooper.'

'Will do, boss. No sweat.'

'And keep your eyes and ears open for any Argentinian patrols.'

'It doesn't have to be said, boss. Good luck.'

'Same to you.'

After a brief exchange of banter from their closest friends, notably Andrew and Jock, Gumboot and Taff were left behind while the other members of the Squadron continued their march through the dark, wind-blown, freezing night.

Two and a half miles on, having met no opposition from the enemy, Jock led them to positions that gave a clear, moonlit view of the aircraft on that narrow strip of land thrusting into the sea. The lights of camp-fires burned all around the airstrip and along the front of the ammunition and supply dumps, carelessly giving away the Argentinian positions where the uniformed sentries, though armed, did not appear to be too attentive. It was almost like being offered a gift.

'Beautiful!' Parkinson whispered, back in action at last. 'Those Argie sentries look comatose. We're going to take them out, gentlemen.'

Signalling silently with his free hand, he motioned the third, reserve group to take cover as best they could, then sent the first group off in various directions, as previously instructed, to seal off the approaches to the airstrip. When they had gone, he nodded at Jock, who signalled 'Follow me' by swinging his right hand into his hip, then led the assault group closer to the airstrip – not quite as far as his OP, but near to where he and the others had been forced to crawl belly-down on the ground.

Moving in for the attack, with speed more important than safety, the assault group advanced at the crouch, weapons at the ready. When they were less than 300 yards from the airstrip, which was within the firing range of their LAWS, M203 grenade-launchers, and other small arms, Parkinson signalled them to prepare for the engagement, then he contacted the fleet on the radio system. Using the designated code, he told them to commence the covering barrage without delay. Receiving confirmation, he handed the phone back to Paddy Clarke.

'Get in contact with the mortar crew,' he said, 'and give them compass bearings. I want them to start firing immediately.'

'Yes, boss,' Paddy said.

Resting on one knee, Parkinson raised his right hand, preparing to give the signal to open fire. Behind him, the assault squadron were also kneeling and taking aim with their wide range of small arms. At the same time, the troopers with the 66mm LAWS extended the 90cm tube, removed the protective cap from each end of the launcher, thus making the folding sights pop up, held the launcher against the shoulder and prepared to press the trigger switch.

For a full minute, each second an eternity, the assault group knelt there in the darkness, wrapped in silence. The first sound was a high, keening wail that came from the direction of the sea, reached a climax right over the airstrip, and was cut off abruptly when the para-flares fired from the *Glamorgan*'s guns exploded noisily, spectacularly, to illuminate the airstrip below.

Major Parkinson instantly dropped his hand – and the assault group opened up on the Pucaras with their small arms.

Almost simultaneously, the first of the bombs from the L16 ML 81mm mortar fired by Gumboot and Taff, two and a half miles away, from compass bearings given over the radio by Paddy, exploded between the Pucaras in a fountain of fire, smoke and bellowing, erupting soil.

Paddy was bawling a revised calibration into the phone as the troopers pressed the triggers of their LAWs, sending rockets racing like tracers into the same area. Other troopers opened fire with their GPMGs, peppering the area with 200 rounds per minute.

Explosions from all these sources erupted

between the aircraft as the Argentinian sentries, taken by surprise, either ran for cover or instinctively fired back with rifles and other automatic weapons.

Hit by a LAW shell fired by Andrew, one of the Pucaras exploded, with pieces of metal and perspex flying in all directions and the cockpit engulfed in crackling, vivid-yellow flames.

Even as this spectacular strike illuminated the area, more air-burst shells were exploding overhead. Also, mortar explosions from the rounds being fired two and a half miles away were erupting between the aircraft to crater the runway.

In the silvery, flickering, artificial light, and with air-burst shells from the fleet, as well as the mortar bombs, causing further havoc, the Argentinians were forced to take cover, running back to their slit trenches at the edge of the airstrip, and aiming only occasional bursts of inaccurate machine-gun fire at the SAS.

'Let's go!' Major Parkinson bawled, boldly leading his men on to the dispersal areas. There, even as they were being fired on, with bullets tearing up concrete in jagged lines all around them, they ran from one plane to the other, coolly rigged explosives to those not already being destroyed with LAW rounds and vicious bursts from the GPMGs, placing the charges to destroy front undercarriages and nose-cones housing avionic equipment.

When the charges exploded, the nose-cones were blown off and the undercarriages demolished, causing the planes to tilt forward with their smashed noses deep in the ground and smoke belching from them.

As the troopers were thus engaged, more shells from the fleet's barrage were falling farther away, making the ground erupt in a series of explosions directly in front of the enemy's defensive positions, eventually striking the base's petrol store and ammunition dump.

Both buildings exploded spectacularly, with searing yellow, red and blue flames stabbing vividly through black, oily smoke. This billowed skyward, then was carried back on the wind to blanket and choke the Argentinian troops. While the Argentinians were temporarily blinded, the last of the charges rigged to the Pucaras by Parkinson's men exploded one by one, causing more flames, smoke and flying debris as the men backed away.

Making his escape beside Major Parkinson, under cover of an arc of continuous fire from Ricketts's SLR, young Danny glanced back over his shoulder, practically skidded to a stop – thus halting Parkinson – and turned back to the airstrip.

'One of the Pucaras is still untouched!' he shouted.

'Damn!' Parkinson exclaimed.

'Bugger that for a joke!' Danny said, then ran back to the planes, ignoring the Argentinian troops, who, in their smoke-wreathed slit trenches, were recovering from their shock and clambering out to spread across the airstrip, firing directly at him. The ground was erupting around him in jagged lines of spitting earth as he raced back to the untouched aircraft, Parkinson and Ricketts right behind him, both firing their SLRs on the move.

Some of the Argentinians went down, spinning like skittles, collapsing, even as Paddy Clarke, still on the PRC 319 radio system, corrected the mortar being fired two and a half miles away and the next rounds, looping in with more accuracy, landed spot on, the explosions throwing the broken bodies of the enemy soldiers high in the air. They fell back like rag dolls, hitting the ground with dreadful force, sometimes practically bouncing off it and appearing to shrivel up where they lay, some visibly scorched and still smouldering, all with broken or crushed bones.

Reaching the untouched Pucara, Danny expertly rigged the explosive charge, under the protective fire of Parkinson and Ricketts. He then waved them away and dropped back to the ground just as some Argentinians rushed at him. Resting on one knee, ignoring the bullets whistling around him and thudding into the Pucara, he fired his SLR with cool, murderous accuracy, downing the four men advancing on him. He then jumped up and fled from the aircraft.

It exploded behind him with a deafening roar. The shock from the blast punched him forward, throwing him face down on the strip. A wave of intense heat swept over him, momentarily suffocating him, then mercifully faded away. He jumped back to his feet and continued racing back to his own men, who were keeping up a relentless barrage of fire as they backed away from the airstrip.

When Danny reached them, stopping between Parkinson and Ricketts, he studied the airstrip and counted eleven blazing, smouldering aircraft.

'Terrific,' he said.

Parkinson checked his wristwatch. The attack had lasted fifteen minutes. He raised his right hand above his head and bawled, 'That's it, men! *Move out!*'

Still keeping up a protective wall of fire, the men backed away from the Argentinians advancing across the airstrip, weaving left and right between the blazing aircraft and the many explosions from the mortars. In the brilliant, silvery light from the air-burst shells they looked faceless, insubstantial, almost ghostlike.

Suddenly, from the direction of the blazing petrol and ammunition dump, a truck filled with Argentinian troops raced at the retreating men.

Jock appeared from nowhere, running back to the strip. He dropped to one knee, raising a 66mm LAW to his shoulder. The ground nearby erupted, hit by a mortar shell, and he was thrown down, rolling over a couple of times, as the smoke swirled about him.

When he sat upright, shaking his head, slapping his own face to help himself recover, his clothes were torn by shrapnel, with blood leaking from wounds to his face and body.

The truck was still racing at him. His fellow troopers poured fire at it. Grimly determined, Jock wiped blood from his face, adopted the kneeling position, removed the protective cap from each end of the launcher, held the weapon against his shoulder, then aimed along the pop-up sights. When he pressed the trigger switch, the backblast made him jerk violently, but the rocket shot straight to its target, creating a stream of flame, and the truck, which was almost on top of him, was hit and blew up. Careening sideways with a squealing of brakes, it crashed into a blazing Pucara, which also exploded.

Though covered in blood, Jock climbed to his feet and made his way unsteadily back to his mates.

Argentinian soldiers jumped out of the truck, some on fire, screaming hideously, flapping at their own burning bodies with smouldering hands. Some of the SAS troopers were undecided what to do about these unfortunates, but young Danny stepped forward, his angelic features highlighted ethereally by the flames, and cut them down in a hail of withering fire from his SLR.

'Put 'em out of their misery,' he explained, turning back to his mates. 'Only thing to do.'

'Yeah,' Andrew said. 'Right.'

'Pull back!' Parkinson shouted, waving his right hand. 'Let's move it! *Go!*'

As the assault group withdrew from the blazing, smoking airstrip, still under cover of mortar fire and naval support from the *Glamorgan*, some brave Argentinians attempted another counter-attack, emerging from the smoke swirling across the strip and firing their weapons. Still kneeling on the ground behind his powerful GPMG, big Andrew let rip with a 200-round burst that cut some of the men down and forced the others to beat a hasty retreat. Then Andrew jumped up, slung his heavy weapon over his shoulder and followed the rest of the Troop back towards the sea.

A sudden explosion made the ground erupt violently in their midst, hurling one trooper high in the air. Crashing back down in a shower of debris, he hit the ground with a bone-breaking thud. His body actually bounced off the earth before rolling over, the bloody bone of a smashed kneecap thrusting out through torn pants, a white rib exposed through shrapnel-slashed flesh. Mercifully concussed, he made no sound.

'Damn!' Ricketts exclaimed. 'The bastards set off a remote controlled land-mine.'

'Medics!' Parkinson yelled.

As the troopers near the concussed man shook their heads to clear their ears, the medics, who had just been waved away by the bloody Jock, rolled their patient onto a stretcher and then hurried off. The troopers closed in behind them to form a protective wall.

Reaching the summit of the low hill that overlooked the airstrip, Parkinson glanced back to take stock of the situation.

In the still flickering, eerie light of the air-burst shells from the Fleet, all of the eleven Pucaras were either burning or smouldering. Craters littered the runway and the ground between the burning planes, ensuring that the airstrip could not be used in the immediate future. There were many dead bodies.

Satisfied, Parkinson was about to turn away when he heard the steady roar of other GPMGs and small arms from the sea road on one side of the airstrip.

Obviously the SAS troopers in the second group, sent there to seal off the approaches to the runway, were stopping the advance, or flight, of Argentinian troops trying to get along the sea road.

Even as Parkinson was gazing in that direction, a series of explosions sent smoke pouring into the sky in the vicinity of the GPMG and small-arms fire, indicating that someone in the group had called in for support from the *Glamorgan*'s big guns. A few minutes later the sound of battle died away – an indication that the second group had stopped the Argentinians and was now also heading back to the LZ.

'Good men,' Parkinson whispered.

The two-and-a-half mile march back to the location of the mortar base-plate was uneventful. There, they picked up Gumboot and Taff, then proceeded back to the LZ. The Sea Kings returned in time and the Squadron was lifted back to the *Hermes*, where the men had a warm welcome from Captain Grenville. Though disappointed that he had not been on the raid, he was delighted that the invasion could now commence.

12

Jock was the first to be shipped back, but not the last. When the shrapnel had been removed, he was a quiltwork of scars, some left to heal on their own, others stitched up, and no matter which way he turned, he lay on a bed of pain. This did not stop the mocking comments from flying thick and fast when he was visited in the ship's sick bay by other members of the Regiment, shortly before being shipped back to Ascension Island and from there on to England.

'I hear your arse is a hot-spot,' big Andrew said, flashing his teeth.

'Don't worry about the shrapnel in your prick,' Paddy said. 'I'm told that if you can manage a hard-on, the wounds open and the pieces just fall out.'

'That's *if* you can get one,' Gumboot clarified,

'which in Jock's case is an issue of doubt. Can I lend you a hand, Jock?'

'Ha, ha,' Jock responded stiffly, lying there like an Egyptian mummy, wrapped from head to toe in bloody bandages, but refusing to show his pain.

'You look pretty good, all told,' Taff informed him, studying the head-to-toe bandages with an experienced eye. 'Like a babe in swaddling clothes. Red and white becomes you.'

'It's just a pity,' Andrew said, 'that the shrapnel missed your mug. You could do with some rearranging there, so a good chance was missed.'

'Still, you'll get a rest,' young Danny said, being more concerned than the others. 'A nice little trip back to Blighty.'

'Right,' Gumboot said. 'Where they should have pretty nurses instead of these blokes. That should perk you up, mate.'

'Then you might get it up,' Andrew added, 'and the stitches will fall out.'

'Fuck you, Andrew,' Jock said. 'Fuck you all, come to that. I don't have stitches in my arse or dick, so go screw yourselves.'

'Even I can't get *mine* around that far,' Paddy said. 'Though if I could, I'm sure I'd have a good time.'

'Christ,' Jock said, rolling his eyes, 'do I have to endure this?'

'You need visits from friends to cheer you up,' young Danny said solemnly. 'That's why we're here.'

'I'm cheered up,' Jock said. 'Thanks a lot. You can all piss off now.'

'He's so ungrateful,' big Andrew said, glancing around as Sergeant Ricketts entered the sick bay and approached the bed. Ricketts glanced dispassionately at Jock, noting the bloodstains on the bandages, then studied each of the other troopers in turn.

'So what are you pisspots doing here?' he asked.

'Cheering him up,' Andrew said.

'Offering sympathy,' added Gumboot.

'Letting him know we all care,' Taff explained.

'I'll bet,' Ricketts grinned, then turned back to Jock. 'Giving you a hard time, are they?'

'Don't worry, boss, I can take it. You can smell the bullshit before they speak it, so I'm well prepared for it.'

'Good,' Ricketts said. 'It shows you've been well trained. A man who can take any kind of flak. A real SAS trooper.'

'That's me,' Jock said, grinning defiantly from his bed of pain. 'So what's happening, boss?'

'You're being medevacked this morning,' Ricketts told him. 'Cross-decked to another ship that'll take you to Ascension Island, then flown from there back to Blighty, where some sympathetic nurse might give you a hand-job under the sheets. What more could you want?'

'To take part in the invasion,' Jock said.

'Not in your state, Trooper. As for you bullshit artists,' Ricketts said, turning to the men gathered about Jock's bed, 'the British landing at San Carlos Water has been scheduled for the twenty-first. As a diversion, we've been tasked with mounting a raid against the Argies at Darwin, East Falkland. This is scheduled for tomorrow, so we're being cross-decked to the *Intrepid* this evening. I therefore suggest that you go and get your kit in order. Say goodbye to this useless case on the bed, then get the hell out of here. We've no time to waste.'

'Gee, thanks,' Jock said. 'It's nice to know I'm valued.'

'I'll see you back in Hereford,' Ricketts said, 'when you're out of those bandages. You'll be more valued then. Keep your pecker up, Jock.'

'Aye, boss, I'll do that. Best of luck for tomorrow.'

Ricketts nodded, glanced briefly at the other

men, then raised his hand and spread his fingers. 'Five minutes,' he said, then left Jock to the mercy of his comrades.

'You hear that, Jock?' Andrew said. 'You've got to keep your pecker up.'

'I'll go fetch some splints,' Paddy said. 'I think Jock's going to need them.'

'OK, you bunch of shites,' Jock said, 'you've all had your fun. Now piss off and leave me alone. I've got things to think about – like a hand-job from a saucy wee nurse in Hereford while you're getting your balls shot off.'

'There's still life in this corpse,' Andrew said. 'I take that as a hopeful sign.'

'Amen,' Taff added.

Before any more could be said, the medics came in to prepare Jock for his cross-decking. Ordered out of the sick bay, the troopers shook Jock's hand, offered a few more parting shots, then went up to the flight deck to see him off.

Jock was brought up on a stretcher and mocked relentlessly while being carried across the deck to the Sea King. He waved once, weakly but defiantly, before being hoisted up into the helicopter. Then the door was slammed shut and the helo roared into life, creating a wind that whiplashed the watching troopers before lifting off. It hovered above the helipad like an indecisive bird, then ascended and headed south, joining the many other helos already in the air, noisily cross-decking men and supplies from one ship to the other in the build-up for the forthcoming assault on San Carlos Water.

Ricketts, who was leaning against the railing near the helipad, glanced across at the many other ships of the fleet – aircraft-carriers, destroyers, frigates, hospital ships and landing vessels – now gathering together for the definitive assault on the Falkland Islands. Seeing him there, Danny joined him.

'The first of us to be shipped back,' he said, his gaze focused on the helo that was taking Jock back to Ascension Island.

'Yes,' Ricketts replied distractedly. Then he added ominously: 'Let's hope he's the last.'

Two hours after sunset, nearly thirty members of the Squadron, wearing full belt kit and life-jackets, as well as carrying the usual complement of weapons, boarded a Sea King for the five-minute cross-decking from the *Hermes* to the *Intrepid*, now cruising a mere half-mile away. From there, the Troop would be inserted by sea onto Darwin, East Falkland.

Within minutes the helicopter was in the air and heading across the relatively short stretch of dark sea. In the equally dark, cramped passenger compartment of the helo, the noise was deafening and the atmosphere claustrophobic.

'Thing I most dislike about this whole business,' Andrew said, distractedly checking the ammunition belts criss-crossing his chest, 'are these damned chopper flights. Like being in a coffin. Even worse than a chartered flight to Spain. It don't do me no good, man.'

'It's not a chopper,' the Loadmaster said. As it was only a five-minute flight, he was still standing by the door, getting ready to open it. 'It's a *helicopter* – or a *helo*. Get your terminology right, soldier. We don't like the word "chopper".'

'Strike me dead, man, for using the wrong word, but whether it's a helicopter or a helo, I still don't like it, period.'

'You're just scared of heights is all.'

'I can't see no heights, man. I can't see a damned thing. All I can see is your white face in that overhead light there.'

The Loadmaster grinned. 'More than I can see, friend. In the darkness, you're practically invisible. Must be useful in your line of business. Is that why they took you on?'

'Ha, ha, very funny.' Big Andrew was not amused. He ran his fingers up and down his M203 grenade-launcher, then checked that its incendiary bombs were still in the pockets of the belt criss-crossing his chest. 'You want a tan like this, man, you've got to go and cook in the sun. With me it comes natural.'

'So how come you take charter flights to Spain?'

'I like the rain on the plain.'

The Loadmaster laughed and looked out of the window. 'We're about 300 feet up,' he said. 'We'll be coming in to land any minute, so you've no need to fear.'

'That guy's talking to himself,' Andrew said. 'He can't be talking to me. I don't know what fear means. Hey, Danny, have you ever been scared? Do you know what fear is?'

'I think it's RAF slang,' Danny replied. 'They know lots of words we don't.'

Andrew chuckled at that. 'Right on, my little brother. They've got a language all their own. Phrases like "scared shitless" and "crapping your pants" and "turning white around the gills" and so forth – all the things they know from personal experience, right?'

'Right,' Danny said.

Andrew let the Loadmaster hear his healthy

bellow of laughter. He stopped laughing when the Loadmaster listened intently to his earphones, glanced out of the window again, then said with an evil grin: 'Sorry, guys, but we've got a bit of a delay. Another helo's still sitting on the *Intrepid*'s flight deck, so we're going to have to complete a second circuit.'

'What?' Andrew asked. 'Are you putting me on, man?'

'No, Trooper, I'm not putting you on. We're going to have to stay aloft for a while. But don't worry, it's free. Hey, I notice you haven't gone white around the gills yet. Is that a good sign or simply a physical impossibility?'

Andrew rolled his big brown eyes. 'Oh, we've got a clown on board. Someone should give him a clip-on nose and a striped, cone-shaped hat. Another circuit, for Christ's sake!'

Some of the men were still laughing, but they stopped when they heard a very loud, unusual bang.

The noise was still reverberating through the passenger compartment when the helo tilted sharply, throwing the Loadmaster to the floor, scattering the other men and their equipment, then plunged screaming and shuddering towards the ocean.

'We're going down!' someone bawled.

Stars exploded in Ricketts's head when a boot kicked his temple. He opened his eyes to find himself pinned to the floor – or perhaps the ceiling – in a tangle of writhing bodies – men bawling, weapons clanging – as the helo continued its clamorous dive towards the ocean, shuddering wildly, going into a spin, its engines roaring unnaturally, as if about to explode. Ricketts took a deep breath and reached out for his SLR – too late.

The helo plunged into the sea with a dreadful roaring, tearing noise, metal buckling and shrieking before the water poured in, drenching him, completely submerging him, cutting off all sound. Ricketts was picked up, turned over, battered, sent spinning like a top, then smashed against something hard in that terrible silence. He may have blacked out briefly – he couldn't be sure – but consciousness returned with a sudden inrush of noise – splashing water, bawling men, clattering weapons, twanging metal – and he surfaced beneath the tilting ceiling of the helo, coughing water, surrounded by other bobbing heads, drifting webbing and clothing.

'We're turning over!' someone cried out. 'It's starting to sink!'

That much was true. As Ricketts trod water, unable to find the floor beneath him, he saw that the helo was tilting to the side, sinking, with the water pouring in through the smashed perspex of the cockpit, where the pilot, waist-deep in water, the navigator dead beside him, was clambering out, holding a distress flare in his hand.

With only inches between himself and the ceiling – now actually the overturning side – of the helo, Ricketts had to frantically tread water while being dragged under by his ammunition belts and webbing. Out of the corner of his eye, he saw Andrew's wide eyes and flashing teeth; clinging to a door handle, he was tugging young Danny up out of the water to enable him to shuck off the heavy bergen that was dragging him under. Beyond Andrew, in a jagged frame of shattered perspex, silhouetted by the night sky, now outside the helo and balanced precariously on the smashed nose, the pilot was firing his distress flare.

It shot up out of sight with a whoosh, making the pilot's arm jerk and almost throwing him off the nose, then exploded directly above to illuminate the crashed, sinking helo.

Even as Ricketts felt a brief exhilaration, a dead body surfaced near him, then another, and a third, as the helo turned turtle and sank completely. Ricketts saw the pilot waving his arms wildly and toppling off the turning nose. He caught a glimpse of Andrew and Danny falling into one another and plunging into the rising water. Then he too was submerged as the water reached the turning wall, forcing him down into total darkness, silence, and a numbing cold.

He lost all sense of direction, not knowing up from down, but managed to wriggle out of his webbing and get rid of his heavy boots before he ran completely out of breath and again started blacking out. He forced himself to stay calm and resisted unconsciousness.

It was darkness and silence. A bottomless well. Ricketts was only made aware of himself by the objects, or bodies, bumping into him. *Open your eyes*! he thought. It was hard, but he managed it. Objects darker than the darkness of the water were swirling and turning around him. *Dead bodies*, he thought. The sea's darkness was streaked with light . . . *Light? What light?* he wondered. *Where's the light coming from?* His lungs were about to burst. He could hardly think straight. His thoughts went in and out like faulty gears as he slipped towards unconsciousness. *Light*! he said in his shrinking mind. *The light's streaking that water filled with dark shapes.* It was dimly illuminating the bodies bobbing and sinking around him. A light coming from somewhere.

He forced his eyes to stay open, though they stung from the salt water. Numbed by cold, bereft of air, Ricketts was sinking and drifting out of himself when he saw where the light was. It looked like a star, now expanding, now contracting, its striations spreading out all around him like a pale, shivering web in which the dark, drifting objects, the drowned bodies, appeared to be trapped.

Ricketts turned towards the light, fighting oblivion, kicking his legs, and reached out to take hold of the star and let its light warm him. He surfaced to a burst of sound – splashing water, bawling men – and saw that the light was the moon beaming down on the sea.

He had made his escape from the sinking helo by swimming up through the hole in the smashed nose, now sinking below him.

Getting his senses back, he realized that the SARBE surface-to-air rescue beacon – essentially a small radio used for communication between the helo and the ship – had probably kept sending out its distress signal until the helo sank beneath the waves. With luck, an SAR, search and rescue, helicopter would soon be on its way. Meanwhile, like the other survivors bobbing around him, he had to stay afloat and hope to be rescued before suffering from hypothermia or even freezing to death.

As the helo sank, bubbles rose to the surface and the high waves turned into a minor whirlpool that picked Ricketts up and swept him in a circle with the other survivors and debris – mostly webbing and clothing. Wiping the water from his eyes as best he could with numbed fingers, he saw Andrew clinging to a rescue dinghy, its automatic search-and-rescue beacon transmitting while the pilot let off more flares. Beyond them, surprisingly far out to sea, Danny Porter drifted all alone. Between them, and between Andrew and Ricketts, were other survivors. Some of them, badly battered in the crash, were already dying and sinking.

The whirlpool created by the sinking helo subsided, leaving the waves to rise and fall as usual. Picked up on the waves, then swept along in the rushing troughs, Ricketts knew he was safe in his life-jacket. He also knew that he was starting to freeze and could do nothing about it.

The dead and their debris were floating all around him when he saw an SAR helicopter emerging from the darkness, its searchlights beaming down on the sea, to illuminate Danny, floating alone, drifting south towards Antarctica.

Even as the helo descended to just above the surface, its spinning rotors sucking the sea up in angry waves that threatened to submerge Danny before he could grab the unfurling lifeline, the lights of a cutter materialized in the distance, obviously coming from the direction of the fleet and heading steadily for the scene of the crash.

Picked up on a high wave, then sucked down through a trough, Ricketts briefly lost sight of Danny. When he was swept back up on the crest of the same wave, he saw Danny in mid-air, swinging from side to side, being winched up to the SAR helo, unreal in the silvery beam of the searchlights, obscured by spray from the surging sea.

The helo flew back towards the fleet, with Danny being winched up as it went, then disappeared into the darkness, taking Danny with it.

Clinging to the rescue dinghy, but seeing the approaching cutter, the resolute pilot of the crashed helo set off another flare. It exploded high above in a brilliant fireworks display, bathing the black sea in its silvery light. In that eerie glow Ricketts saw the other survivors; he also saw the dreadful debris of the crash, including dead bodies kept adrift by their lifebelts, some staring skyward.

Aware that he was freezing, hardly able to feel his limbs, Ricketts kept moving as best he could. It was, he assumed, like having amputated limbs: he could sense them there and will them to move, but he couldn't really feel them. Nevertheless, he was moving – the splashing water told him that – and he kept doing so until the cutter arrived and started picking the men up.

Ricketts was lucky, being one of the first. Rolling onto the deck and being immediately wrapped in blankets, he couldn't feel a thing – not the deck, not his own body – but experienced an enormous exhilaration. Big Andrew followed shortly after, his face wet and gleaming, groaning, 'Christ, man, I'm cold, so damned cold. What the fuck happened, man?' He was rolled onto a stretcher, covered in blankets, given a brandy, then picked up and carried away with Ricketts, who realized, when he floated up beside Andrew, that he, too, was being carried on a stretcher. He was too numb to feel it.

Ricketts, Andrew and Danny spent the rest of the night in bed in the sick bay, recovering from mild hypothermia and unable to sleep properly because the pain, which was caused by the return of feeling to their limbs, made them too uncomfortable.

Early next morning, when Major Parkinson came to see them, he told them that the cause of the crash was unknown, but that it may have been caused by a large seabird being sucked into an engine intake.

'Whatever the reason,' Parkinson said, 'it's been an absolute disaster. Few of the men made it to the surface. Eighteen are dead. You three were lucky.'

'Is the assault on the Falklands still scheduled?' Ricketts asked.

'Yes, Sergeant, it is.'

'What about the diversionary assault on East Falkland? The one we should have made?'

'That's still scheduled as well. We simply can't let this dreadful incident stop us. The diversion is vital.'

'And us?' Ricketts asked, indicating Andrew and Danny in the adjoining beds.

'Just get some rest, Sergeant.'

Parkinson left the sick bay without saying another word. When he had gone, Andrew turned to Ricketts and said, 'He didn't actually answer the question. What does *that* mean?'

'If it means what I think we won't be happy, but let's wait and see.'

Thirty minutes later, the ship's doctor arrived. After examining his three patients in turn, he said: 'Well, lads, aren't *you* the lucky ones? I'm going to have to ship you back to Hereford for recuperation.'

'What recuperation?' Ricketts asked. 'There's nothing wrong with us, doctor.'

'You're suffering from hypothermia.'

'We *were* suffering from that. It was mild and we're not suffering any more. We don't need to recuperate.'

'Yes, you do, Sergeant. This condition is unpredictable. You could even be suffering from shock without knowing it, so you have to go back.'

'Bullshit,' Ricketts said. 'Feed that birdseed to the others. We were first out of the water and we weren't in it long. Trooper Porter – five minutes. Me – about ten minutes. Trooper Winston – a couple of minutes longer than me, but he's as strong as an ox. We're not suffering from hypothermia, Doc, and we're not going back.'

'You'll all do what you're told, Sergeant Ricketts, and that's all there is to it. Now lie down and shut up.'

'Yes, Doc,' Ricketts said. He waited until the

doctor had left the sick bay, then turned to Andrew and Danny. 'So now you know what Parkinson meant. We're not going to take part in the final assault on the Falkand Islands. We're being dropped from the Task Force and sent home to be mended.'

'Mended?' Andrew responded, outraged. 'Who the fuck needs mending? I'm as fit as a fiddle and raring to go, so I don't need no spell in a hospital in Hereford, tucked up nice and cosy with a bunch of whining wimps and premature geriatrics. Fuck it, man, we've come all this way, doing a good job, and now they're planning to send us back. It's a bag of unwholesome shit.'

'I agree,' Ricketts replied.

'So do I,' Danny said. 'I don't think it's fair at all. I'm already bored lying in this bed and we've only been here one night. I want to be part of the assault and take out some more Argies. We've earned that right, Sarge.'

'How do you feel?' Ricketts asked him.

'The same as always. I'm not suffering from hypothermia, I don't have a temperature, and I've got a lot of energy to burn. I don't want to go back, boss.'

'What's that fucking doctor know?' Big Andrew was working himself into a lather. 'He sits on his arse all day, treating a lot of poncy sailors, sticking thermometers up their arses, probably his swollen dong as well, and expressing sympathy when they say they have a cold or got ill drinking mother's milk. He's a fucking Navy doctor – a soft twat treating wimps. He'd send a sailor back for recuperation if he just stubbed his toe. So who's he to say we're not fit enough to fight? Tell him to go bang a few more sailors and let us get on with it.'

His increasingly venomous monologue was only interrupted when Paddy, Gumboot and Taff – who had not been assigned to the diversionary mission to East Falkland and were therefore hale and hearty – arrived at the sick bay for some mischief. When they saw the grim expression on Ricketts's face, the jibes died on their lips.

'Where are our uniforms?' Ricketts asked.

'In the laundry,' Gumboot informed him. 'Being cleaned and pressed.'

'Since last night?'

'Yes, boss.'

'Then they're ready.'

'I guess so.'

'Go and get those three uniforms, Gumboot, and bring them back here.'

227

'You want your underclothes as well, do you, boss?'

'Don't piss around with me, Gumboot. I want everything – uniforms, underclothes, socks and boots – and I want them right now.'

'I'm on my way, boss.'

Gumboot departed and returned soon enough with the clothing. Ricketts slid out of bed, carelessly washed and dressed himself, combed his dishevelled hair, then marched grimly to the ladies' toilet, still housing the SAS HQ. Major Parkinson was there, leaning over a cluttered table, thoughtfully studying a map of East Falkland with captains Hailsham and Grenville. They all looked up in surprise when Ricketts entered.

'What are you doing here, Sergeant Ricketts?' Parkinson asked. 'I thought you were confined to the sick bay, prior to being flown back to Hereford.'

'I don't want to go back to Hereford, boss. Neither do troopers Winston and Porter. We all want to stay here.'

'What you want is irrelevant, Sergeant. The doc says you must . . .'

'Fuck the doc, boss. He doesn't know shite from shinola. He says we have to go back to recuperate, which is pure bloody nonsense. We were only in that water five minutes and we know how we feel – and we're all feeling fine.'

'I don't give a damn how you feel – you're all going back.'

'No, we're not, boss.'

Parkinson straightened up, glanced at Hailsham and Grenville, then stared unflinchingly at Ricketts. 'You're being insubordinate, Sergeant.'

'What's that mean, boss? That sounds like an RAF or Navy word. It's not a word that I know.'

'A smart ass,' Hailsham said.

'A hard head,' Grenville added.

'A smart-assed hard head,' Parkinson said, 'who's asking for trouble.'

'Him and his troopers,' Hailsham said. 'They're all begging for aggro.'

'Then let's give them a bit of aggro,' Grenville added with a sly grin. 'As much as the bullshit artists can take. It's the least we can do.'

'OK, Sergeant,' Parkinson said, his gaze steady and bright, 'you have heard judgement passed by your superior officers. If it's trouble you want, you can have it.'

'Yes, boss,' Ricketts said.

'We insert tomorrow,' Parkinson told him.

'We're 18 men down, but their replacements are parachuting in tonight. Take care of them, Sergeant.'

'Yes, boss. Thank you, gentlemen.'

A jubilant Ricketts returned to the sick bay, where he eagerly informed Andrew and Danny about the boss's decision. They both raised their clenched fists in the air and let out a loud cheer.

That evening Ricketts, Andrew, Danny, Gumboot and Taff were leaning on the railing of the flight deck, looking out over the calm, moonlit sea as the replacements for the 18 dead jumped out of the tailgate of a Hercules C-130 flying over the fleet. Picked up by the slipstream and spread across the sky, they descended silently on billowing white parachutes, falling silently, gracefully, like pollen in a field at night, to splash one after the other into the sea, rising and falling on foam-capped, murmuring waves.

The replacements popped their life-jackets and floated freely with the tide, waiting patiently for the crew of the Rigid Raiders from the *Hermes* to reach them and pull them to safety.

For a while 18 parachutes drifted like flowers in the black sea.

Eighteen flowers for the 18 dead.

13

The following evening, 60 men of D Squadron landed near Goose Green with GPMGs, a MILAN anti-tank weapon, an American Stinger surface-to-air (SAM) missile system, 81mm mortars, and the usual collection of automatic and semi-automatic rifles, favouring the L1A1 SLR, the Heckler & Koch G3, and the ever-reliable M16. This time their intention was not to hide from the Argentinians, but to let them know they were there and create the impression that a battalion ten times their number had landed.

This would merely be one of several diversions being created that night to distract the enemy's attention from the main landings on the opposite coast, far to the north of Goose Green.

Inserted on East Falkland by Sea King helicopters, the Squadron, led by Major Parkinson and including captains Hailsham and Grenville, embarked on a twenty-four-hour forced march south, across rolling fields of marshy peat and tussock grass whipped constantly by sleet and freezing wind. It was an arduous march offering little respite, but endured with a combination of physical strength and the traditional, though now mostly whispered, bullshit.

'To think you could have escaped this,' Gumboot said to Andrew, 'by letting yourself be shipped back to England and a Hereford rest home. You three must be mad.'

'Dedication, Gumboot. It's a word you won't know. One used by the kind of individual who stands too tall for you to see.'

'Wanking again, are you, Andrew? Tugging that big, purple dong. In real terms I stand taller than you by a mile and a half, so your size doesn't bother me.'

'You mean the size of his purple dong?'

'No, Paddy, I don't. I'm talking about real stature, my friend, though that's a word *you* won't understand.'

'I befriend him and he turns on me. Insults my intelligence. In fact, I once saw a statue in a museum – a naked man with a white dong. I was only a teenager, on an outing with my school class, and the size of the dong on that stature gave me problems for years.'

'It's not the size – it's the quality,' Taff advised with a solemn nod.

'I learnt that too late in life,' Paddy explained, 'which is why I lack stature like my friend here – the Jock with the fantastic vocabulary of words he can't actually spell.'

'You must be talking about Andrew,' Jock said. 'He's the one with the banana-republic education and the need to assert himself. Now me, I'm white as snow with no hang-ups . . .'

'Which is why he stands tall,' Andrew interjected, 'though only five foot five inches in stature. Who the fuck's kidding whom?'

'Quiet back there,' Ricketts said, trying to glance over his shoulder, one eye visible around the edge of his packed bergen and gleaming in the darkness. 'Keep your voices down. You're not supposed to be a bunch of car salesmen, advertising your presence. Zip your lips and pick those feet up. We've a long way to go yet.'

'Yes, boss!' they chorused in a whisper, then did as they were told, leaning into the wind, forcing themselves to go faster, marching throughout the night, resting up before dawn, having a breakfast of cold snacks and water, helping the grass grow with their urine and excrement, then moving on again, into the day's sleet-filled grey light, marching, ever marching, towards the horizon and what lay beyond. Twenty-four hours later, back in early morning's darkness, exhausted but not defeated and still raring to go, they arrived at the Argentinian garrison.

Remarkably, it was brightly illuminated, its defensive slit trenches clearly visible in the lights beaming out of the many huts raised behind them. The sentries, placed well ahead of the trenches, were completely exposed.

'Looks like they're not expecting us,' Parkinson whispered.

'So let's give them a little surprise,' Grenville replied.

'Why not?' Hailsham asked.

After dividing the Squadron into three groups – one led by Hailsham, another by Grenville and the third by himself – Parkinson spread them out over a wide arc as part of his strategy for making the Argentinians believe that they were being attacked by a vastly greater number of men. When the 80 troopers were all in place, Parkinson contacted the *Ardent*, out at sea, requesting that the previously agreed support barrage from its single 4.5in gun be implemented immediately. After the ship had confirmed, Parkinson knelt beside Ricketts and waited.

'Here goes,' Parkinson whispered.

Ricketts merely showed his crossed fingers and gave a broad grin.

The sound of the *Ardent*'s big gun was heard by the Squadron as a distant, muffled boom. Hardly more than a second later the first shell exploded with a mighty roar and the ground erupted in front of the Argentinian slit trenches.

Immediately Parkinson dropped his arm, letting his group open fire with everything they had, including mortars and small arms, causing another shocking, deafening din. Simultaneously Paddy Clarke, as signaller, relayed the firing command to the other two groups, thus releasing a barrage of fire along an arc at least half a mile wide and angled towards the Argentinian positions, as if about to surround them.

Between the *Ardent*'s single gun and the mortars, explosions were now taking place all over the field in front of the enemy positions. Meanwhile the troopers were firing their small arms without letting up. Even before the Argentinians could gather their senses enough to return fire,

Paddy had given new calibrations to the mortars placed farther back. Soon shells were falling between and behind the slit trenches.

Eventually, with mortar and big-gun shells exploding along the length of the Argentinian positions, filling the air with flying soil and wreathing the area in smoke, the enemy returned fire with their small arms.

Noting this, Parkinson had Paddy contact the other two groups by radio and order them to start changing positions, moving even farther apart, to convince the enemy that the line of attack was much wider and involved at least a full battalion.

Even as Paddy did so, and while Sergeant Ricketts was fitting the MILAN anti-tank weapon to its tripod, big Andrew was expertly raking the slit trenches with automatic fire from his roaring GPMG.

Having set up the MILAN, Ricketts lay behind it, beside Taff Burgess, who already was squinting down into its optical sight. Getting the target centred in his thermal-imaging sight, which would bring the SACLOS semi-automatic guidance system into play, Taff placed one hand firmly over the carry handle, to hold the MILAN steady, then carefully pressed the trigger grip.

The backblast rocked his body, as if tugging him off the ground, and the anti-tank missile shot out of the exit point and raced on a plume of fire-streaked smoke towards the enemy position. The ground erupted just in front of the prefabricated buildings lined up behind the slit trenches, filling the air with billowing smoke and showering the men in the trenches with raining soil.

'Too short,' Ricketts said.

'Give me a chance,' Taff replied. 'The next one won't be too short, boss. Just hold on to your hat.'

Glancing across the field, Ricketts saw that the Argentinians, though returning the SAS fire, had still not left their trenches.

'It's working,' he said to Major Parkinson. 'They obviously think we're a whole battalion and they're scared to come out.'

'Let's hope it stays that way,' Parkinson said.

More shells from the mortars and another from the *Ardent* caused havoc to the Argentinian defensive trenches, the air above and in front of them filled with smoke, raining soil and debris.

Smiling dreamily, Taff inserted another missile with folded wings into the launcher tube of the MILAN, squinted down into the optical sight, centred his target and pressed the trigger grip.

The backblast was deafening and rocked him again, but this time he was on target and one of the buildings behind the slit trenches was hit, exploding in flames, its roof being blown off, the walls collapsing in on the flames and causing a great shower of sparks.

'Good one, Taff,' Ricketts said.

'Damn right, it's a good one,' Taff replied. 'Right on the nose, boss!'

Hot debris from the explosion rained down on the slit trenches as some Argentinian troops, screaming in agony, tried to climb out. Big Andrew, monolithic behind his GPMG, cut them down with a short, precise burst. The Argentinians threw up their arms as soil and dust spat about them. They jerked and shook epileptically, toppled over in all directions, hit the ground beneath the still showering debris or rolled back down into the trenches.

'Take that, you cunts,' Andrew hissed, continuing to rake the area with murderous fire as young Danny, right beside him, methodically picked off single targets with his SLR, whispering, 'One, two, three', as he did so, like a kid playing marbles in the schoolyard, counting them off as he hit them, the number growing each time. The Argentinians were falling like flies, but they didn't seem real from where he was.

'The rest are still keeping their heads down,' Ricketts observed. 'They think we're here in our hundreds.'

Parkinson checked his wristwatch. 'Good,' he said. 'Paddy, get me HQ on that radio.' Handed the phone, he plugged his free ear with his finger, to cut out the ferocious noise of the battle taking place on both sides and to the front, then listened intently to what he was being told by HQ on the *Hermes*.

Passing the phone back, he said: 'The invasion of the Falklands has commenced. *Fearless* and *Intrepid* are anchored off Jersey Point, West Falkland, with the troops already disembarked from the LCUs and advancing inland. *Brilliant*, *Canberra*, *Norland*, *Fort Austin* and *Plymouth* are anchored in the Falkland Straits. The *Antrim*'s guns are shelling Fanning Head in support of the landings there. More ships are presently steaming into San Carlos Water and Port Stanley is under constant air attack. This is it, gentlemen.'

Again taking the phone, Parkinson contacted the other two groups, led by Hailsham and Grenville, told them the news, then ordered them to spread out even more and continue the mock assault on the Darwin defences. That they did so was soon indicated by the increased size of the arc of fire, which now seemed at least a mile long.

Parkinson moved his own men, then moved them again, and kept doing this as the others were doing the same. They kept this up throughout the morning, never letting up on their fire, and the Argentinians, obviously thinking that they were being attacked by a full battalion, returned the fire in a confused, desultory manner, but never left their slit trenches.

By the hour before dusk the three groups had advanced and spread out until they were practically forming an immense semicircle around the burning, smoking enemy defences. Keeping contact by radio, Parkinson told them to keep firing until dawn, then advance under cover of the morning's remaining darkness and meet up at their chosen grid location well north of the confused Argentinian troops.

By this time, too, he had learned from constant radio communication with the fleet that 12 British ships were now in the Falkland Straits, another five warships were patrolling just outside, and the landing troops, including

40 Commando and 2 Para, were occupying Port San Carlos and Ajax Bay.

By the early hours of the following morning, when the three SAS groups had stopped firing, circled around the blazing, smoking Argentinian positions, and met up north of Darwin, to embrace each other, shake hands and settle down to a good breakfast, the landings on the opposite coast had been a complete success and the battle for the Falkland Islands was well under way.

14

'I'm proud to say,' Major Parkinson informed his troops when they had gathered north of Darwin, though still in sight of the smoke rising from the burning buildings of the Argentinian garrison, 'that the British landing troops were guided in by the torches of the SBS already ashore and hiding out in OPs. Congratulations, Captain Grenville.'

'Thanks, boss. They knew what they were doing. Now what about the 80 men we have here? What do we do with them?'

'Create havoc,' Parkinson said. 'We break up into 16 groups of five, all heading north, but each covering different areas, and we gradually make our way to Port Stanley, harassing the enemy in whatever way we can – wherever we can.'

'Sounds good to me,' Captain Hailsham said.

'Keep the Argies dancing on tiptoe, turning left and right.'

'Hit and run,' Parkinson said. 'Disorientation and confusion. Outside the normal chain of command. All the way to Port Stanley.'

'Naughty, but nice,' Grenville said.

'Better than sitting here waiting to be lifted out,' Captain Hailsham added. 'A positive contribution.'

'Might cause a little annoyance at HQ,' Grenville reminded them.

'Who dares wins,' Parkinson said with a grin.

Pleased with themselves, they divided the men into 16 groups of five, with Parkinson getting Sergeant Ricketts and troopers Winston, Porter and Gillis, the latter acting as signaller.

With one man placed in charge of each group, the teams were given individual grid references before moving off in open formation, all heading north, but in slightly different directions, thus gradually losing sight of one another in the broad, mist-wreathed fields.

Soon Parkinson and his team were all alone in the visible landscape, marching in file formation, with Danny well in front, taking the 'point' as lead scout, Parkinson second in line as PC, Gumboot third as signaller, Ricketts protecting

Gumboot, and Andrew, heavily burdened with an American Stinger SAM system, as well as his GPMG and packed bergen, bringing up the rear as Tail-end Charlie.

By nine that morning they learnt from Gumboot's radio that the only casualty during the landing at San Carlos Water was the loss of three Royal Marines air-crew, forced down when fired on by enemy ground forces. However, over the next hour they saw many Argentinian aircraft, including Pucaras, Skyhawks and Daggers, flying from the mainland and Port Stanley, towards the sea and back, obviously attacking the fleet and the landing force.

The sound of bombing was clear even from where they were marching, now farther north of Darwin, though they were encouraged to learn, both visually and from Gumboot's radio, that Port Stanley and the enemy positions around it were being attacked relentlessly by Sea Harriers dropping air-burst shells and 1000lb bombs, as well as by Vulcans firing American Shrike radiation-homing missiles. The smoke darkening the sky on the horizon was boiling up from Port Stanley.

After a four-hour march, the men had encountered no enemy forces, though they had seen an enormous build-up in the number of British aircraft heading to and from Port Stanley. Stopping for a light lunch of biscuits, chocolate and water, Parkinson checked the southern landscape through binoculars and saw troops advancing across the high ground south of San Carlos Water. Giving Gumboot the grid location and asking him to check on the radio, he was informing that the advancing troops belonged to 2 Para.

'They'll capture what's left of Darwin,' he told Ricketts. 'This advance won't be stopped now. Come on, let's get moving.'

The farther north they advanced, the closer they came to the many inland Argentinian positions, including airstrips. For this reason, flights of enemy aircraft to and from the sea increased, and grew ever closer, the harsh, relentless chatter of their automatic weapons soon adding to the distant noise of exploding bombs.

Late that afternoon they heard over the radio that in San Carlos Water, now dubbed 'Bomb Alley', their support ship, the *Ardent*, had been sunk, the *Argonaut* crippled, and the *Antrim*, *Brilliant* and *Broadsword* all hit by enemy bombs, each suffering different degrees of damage, most of it serious. Also, one Sea Harrier and two helicopters had been lost. In return, 12 Argentinian aircraft had been destroyed and the British force, having gained a foothold on the Falklands, was poised to break out and advance on Port Stanley.

Parkinson and his four men spent that first night in a star-shaped OP, taking turns to sleep, listening to the distant sounds of relentless bombing and assiduously keeping notes on the movements and frequency of Argentinian aircraft. No enemy troops were seen, so at first light they filled in the OP and moved out again, continuing their long march to Port Stanley, following the bleak, windswept coastline.

By dusk they had still seen no enemy troops, so they built an OP and spent another night listening to the radio, sleeping in turn and observing the movements of enemy aircraft.

By dawn they were on the move again, all alone in the vast landscape, but still hearing the sounds of battle in the distance and seeing enemy aircraft flying to and from Port Stanley. During a break for lunch, again cold snacks and water, they learnt from the radio that three more British ships had been hit by Argentinian bombs and Exocet AM.39 missiles, two already sunk, the third sinking.

'The Argentinians are being foolish,' Major Parkinson said. 'They're concentrating all their attacks on the warships in Falkland Sound while ignoring the landing and supply ships. No wonder our troops are advancing with relative ease.'

'I'm glad to hear it,' Ricketts replied.

'I just wish we'd run into some Argies,' young Danny said. 'I'm bored just wandering about here.'

'Right, man,' Andrew said. 'I agree with that sentiment.'

'A right pair of bloody warmongers, you two,' Gumboot informed them. 'Always after the action.'

'It's in the blood,' Andrew retorted. 'We're the sons of the Regiment. Come on, Argies, where the hell are you? I want to cop me an Argie!'

He got his wish soon enough.

Just before dusk they arrived at a lonely farmhouse in a wind-blown valley between Fitzroy and Bluff Cove, with the sea of Port Pleasant Bay visible beyond the edge of the distant cliff. Signalling for the others to drop to the ground, Parkinson, also belly-down, examined the farmhouse through his binoculars.

A single track snaked from the horizon, across that desolate valley of gorse, to the lonely farmhouse. An enemy troop truck was parked in front of it. Smoke was rising from its chimney, indicating that the fire inside was being used. Armed soldiers were wandering casually in and out by the front door, some drinking from mugs. Between Parkinson's group and the house, but well away from it, an Argentinian private was standing guard – though he was in fact sitting on an upturned bucket, smoking a cigarette, distractedly studying his own feet instead of the landscape, his rifle resting carelessly on his crossed legs.

'A sitting duck,' Danny whispered.

'That's a mobile radio patrol,' Parkinson said, noting the makeshift antenna on the roof of the house. 'They're probably using that place as an OP – making daily trips around the area, reporting back what they learn about our troop movements. I don't think we should let them.'

'Absolutely not,' Ricketts replied.

'Let's take it.' Parkinson lowered his binoculars and rubbed his tired eyes. 'Trooper Porter?'

'Yes, boss,' Danny replied, not even having to ask, knowing exactly what was expected and already unstrapping his bergen, to lower it to the ground and leave himself free to move easily. This done, he removed his Fairburn-Sykes commando knife from its sheath, held it firmly in his right hand, then advanced crouched low, with the stealth of a cat, dropping down and rising up and running crouched low again, until he was coming around, then behind, the unsuspecting guard.

Meanwhile, as big Andrew was unslinging his GPMG and holding it across his upturned left arm in the Belfast cradle, Ricketts and Gumboot were covering the distant house with their M16s.

The unwary guard was still studying his booted feet, his clothes flapping in the moaning wind, when Danny rose up behind him, as silent and insubstantial as a wisp of smoke, to slide one hand over his mouth, blocking off all sound, and slash his jugular with the commando knife.

The guard quivered like a bowstring and kicked out with one leg, but Danny dragged him off the bucket and pulled him down to the ground before he could make any sound or further movement. They both vanished in the gorse, Danny on top of his victim, waiting for his final, despairing breath and the stillness of death.

Eventually Danny reappeared, resting on his

knees, waving inward with his raised right hand, signalling the rest of them forward.

'Fucking great!' Andrew whispered.

Still cradling the GPMG, he advanced to where Danny was waiting for him. There, ignoring the dead man, he fixed the machine-gun to its tripod, checked the alignment and prepared to fire on the farmhouse. Changing his mind, he signalled to the others, now coming up behind him, to take cover again, which they did by lying belly-down on the ground. Andrew then clipped his M203 grenade-launcher to the underside of the barrel of his M16, slid the barrel forward and loaded the grenade, then stood up in full view of the enemy troops milling about in front of the farmhouse.

One of the Argentinians looked across the field, directly at Andrew, just as he took the firing position, squinted along the pop-up sight of the M203, braced himself by spreading his thick legs, and fired the grenade.

The Argentinian shouted a warning and threw himself to the ground as the backblast rocked even Andrew's huge bulk and the grenade smashed through a window of the house, sending glass everywhere. The grenade exploded a second later, blowing the other windows out, as Ricketts, Danny and Gumboot opened fire with their M16s, raking the front of the farmhouse, cutting down the few Argentinians who had been too shocked to throw themselves to the ground. The other soldiers started crawling back to the house, where the walls were spitting concrete, but Andrew fired his M203 again, and this time, when the grenade exploded inside the house, it ignited some form of gas – either a cooker or a container – and yellow flames curled out through the windows, clawing at the darkening sky.

The front door burst open and some men rushed out, screaming and slapping at their burning uniforms. They either collapsed of their own accord, rendered unconscious by pain, or were cut down by the semi-automatic fire of the M16s. Then big Andrew placed his M203 on the ground, knelt behind the machine-gun, and proceeded to rake the front of the house, left to right, up and down, until the wall was a living thing, spitting concrete and dust, and the men on the ground in front, trying to crawl back indoors, became whirling dervishes in clouds of exploding soil, their screams lost in the clamour.

Parkinson raised his right hand and waved it in a forward direction, indicating 'Advance'. As Andrew changed the belt in the GPMG, Ricketts, Danny and Gumboot followed Parkinson across the field to the farmhouse, all still firing their weapons as they advanced. Reaching the troop truck, which remained untouched, they saw that the Argentinians in front of the house were either dead or close to it. Some were badly scorched, others soaked in their own blood. The few still alive would not live long and were scratching instinctively at the earth, needing something to cling to.

Knowing that Andrew was keeping them covered, Parkinson led the others into the house. It was a mess. The fragmentation grenades had caused utter havoc, with dead Argentinians peppered with shrapnel, the walls scorched, floorboards torn up and splintered, and the flames, still flickering out through the windows, coming from a punctured portable gas container used for the stove. The Argentinian radio equipment, also badly damaged in the explosions, was sparking and smoking.

'No more messages through that,' Parkinson said with satisfaction. 'No tales about the British advance. A job well done, men.' He went to the table in the middle of the room, which was covered in papers, some of them starting to curl at the edge from the heat of the flames. Flipping through them, at first carelessly, then more intently, he said: 'Well, well, what have we here?' He picked the papers up and waved them in front of Ricketts. 'Precise details of the Argentinian defences. These could be useful. I don't think we can hang around here, Sergeant. We have to get to Port Stanley. That truck outside was untouched, I believe?'

'Yes, boss.'

'Then let's take it. We can get to Port Stanley earlier than planned and set up an OP. However, first I've got to talk to HQ and give them this info.'

After leading them back outside, Parkinson told Ricketts to give Andrew the all-clear, which the latter did with a hand signal. As Andrew was packing up his GPMG and walking up to join them, Parkinson wandered around the front of the house, checking the Argentinian dead and wounded, all of whom were covered in dust and mud. The wounded, however, continued to moan and claw at the earth.

'Let's put them out of their misery,' Baby Face said, stroking the knife sheathed on his hip.

'No, Trooper,' Parkinson said. 'Let's attend to them.'

'There's only the five of us here, boss. We don't have any medics.'

'We have our personal first-aid kits.'

'For personal use, boss. Besides, these men are pretty badly wounded; we can't do much for them.'

'We can stop their bleeding and give them morphine,' Parkinson said. 'Don't shit me, Trooper.'

'Sorry, boss,' Danny said. He glanced at Gumboot, who just shrugged, then withdrew his first-aid kit from his bergen. The others did the same and they all pooled their first-aid kits. Gumboot, who was well trained in medical emergencies, began patching up the Argentinian wounded as best he could as Andrew joined them, setting his GPMG on the ground and flexing his fingers.

'That's some heavy fucker,' he said, 'though she's well worth the effort. What are *you* doing, Gumboot?'

'Patching up these wounded Argies.'

'What the hell for? Those are *our* first-aid kits, man!'

'You don't like it, Trooper?' Major Parkinson asked.

'Just passin' a comment, boss.'

'Weren't you trained in first-aid, Trooper?'

'Sure enough, boss.'

'Then take over from Trooper Gillis. I need

him to stay with me on that radio. Gumboot, get in touch with HQ. Trooper Winston is going to play doctor. He's a man in a million.'

'Sure am, boss,' big Andrew said, looking disgusted. 'Right on, boss, I'm in there.'

Danny stood guard by the truck while Andrew reluctantly patched up the Argentinian wounded, Ricketts gave them cigarettes and water, and Parkinson, with the help of Gumboot, contacted HQ on the *Hermes* and relayed the information he had found in the papers of the enemy patrol. HQ expressed their thanks. They did no more than that. Though the information would hasten the reconquest of Port Stanley, its source would never be revealed. Parkinson and his men were not supposed to be here, so officially they weren't here.

'Thank you, boss,' Parkinson said over the radio to his superior aboard the *Hermes*. 'Over and out.' Handing the phone back to Gumboot, he glanced back over his shoulder at Andrew, still patching up the Argentinian casualties, and asked. 'How are they?'

'Not good, boss. Fucked, actually. No minor wounds here. I've patched them up and filled them with morphine, but they need more attention.'

'We can't take them with us,' Parkinson said, 'so let's leave them some food and water and send someone back later.'

'You're too kind, boss.'

'These poor sods didn't ask for this war. They're just like you and I, Trooper.'

'We're a bit short on food and water ourselves, boss.'

'You're a member of the Regiment, Trooper, and should rise to a challenge.'

'Yes, boss, I hear you.'

In fact the few surviving Argentinians were so badly wounded, so deeply in shock, that they could hardly mutter their thanks when the SAS troopers each contributed half of their rations to a small food-well for them. Ricketts threw in a couple of extra packets of cigarettes as Major Parkinson was climbing up into the front of the Argentinian troop truck and the rest of the men were getting into the back. Ricketts waved goodbye to the dust-covered, moaning Argentinians, then he climbed up into the driver's seat of the truck, beside Major Parkinson, and drove off, the truck bouncing and rattling along the muddy, wind-whipped road, heading for the stormy horizon way past Bluff Cove.

'This will save us boot leather as well as

time,' Major Parkinson said. 'It's so nice to go travelling.'

'I'll second that,' Ricketts said.

They drove through the night and stopped just before dawn, well on the road to Port Stanley. Breakfasting on the last of their meagre dry rations – the rest had been given to the wounded Argentinians – they learned over the radio that the enemy garrisons at Darwin and Goose Green, psychologically destroyed by the SAS diversionary raid, had fallen to the 2nd Parachute Regiment, with 1300 Argentinians taken prisoner. Since then, the 550 Marines of 42 Commando had yomped eastward, all the way from Ajax Bay on San Carlos Water, to Teal Inlet, about ten miles north-west of Port Stanley, which they had secured with the aid of SBS teams already placed there.

'Another medal for Captain Grenville,' Parkinson said with a smile of pleasure and pride. 'OK, men, let's go.'

They had only been driving for thirty minutes, into increasingly hilly terrain, when they were attacked by a British Sea Harrier. Flying in from the west, obviously engaged in an inland recce, the pilot could not resist a lone Argentinian troop truck and swept in low to rake it with his guns.

Momentarily forgetting that he was driving an enemy truck, Ricketts was shocked by the attack, accelerated automatically, then realized what was happening and slammed on the brakes, thus throwing the vehicle into a skid, with the men in the rear tumbling about and bawling. Careering across the road, the truck ploughed into soft earth, bounced up and down, shuddered violently and came to rest, as the Harrier roared directly overhead and away again, its bullets still stitching lines of spitting soil across the field by the road.

'Shit!' Ricketts exclaimed, opening his door and dropping down to the ground as Major Parkinson did the same and the other men jumped out of the rear, not forgetting to throw their kit and weapons out first.

'Take cover!' Major Parkinson shouted. 'Get as far away from the truck as possible. He's coming back! *Go now*!'

True enough, the Sea Harrier was completing a great circle in the sky above the Atlantic, beyond the edge of the field.

The men scattered as it returned, first seeming to glide, then rushing and roaring at them, its guns roaring also, the bullets preceding the aircraft by creating lines of spitting soil that raced across the field and peppered the truck, including the petrol tank, making it explode with a godalmighty clamour.

Ricketts and the others were just throwing themselves to the ground when the truck's doors were blown off, its tyres burst into flames and melted instantaneously, and its canvas top became a great bonfire under a mushroom of oily smoke. The Harrier had already ascended and disappeared in the distance when the truck, already a blackened shell wreathed in flame and smoke, hiccuped from internal convulsions and collapsed onto wheels devoid of tyres, the melted rubber still smouldering.

'Shit!' Ricketts exclaimed again.

'There goes our transport,' Gumboot said.

'A British Harrier!' Andrew burst out. 'I don't fuckin' believe it!'

'OK, men,' Major Parkinson said, climbing back to his feet and wiping the earth from his Gore-tex jacket, 'if we must yomp, we must. Pick up your kit and let's go. No point staying here.'

'Yes, boss,' Danny said.

Falling automatically into single file, in the usual order, they continued their march to Port

Stanley. Now crossing the empty fields between Bluff Cove and Sapper Hill, they were seeing more aircraft, both British and Argentinian, as well as hearing the sounds of battle more clearly. There was smoke in the distant sky, boiling up from the horizon, and they knew that it was coming from Port Stanley, now being bombed daily.

Later that afternoon, they were attacked by another aircraft, this time an Argentinian Pucara that roared out of nowhere, all guns firing, stitching the earth all around them, then flew off again and circled to come back. Now mad as hell, big Andrew removed his American Stinger SAM system from where it was strapped to his bergen, inserted a missile canister armed with a 3kg high-explosive fragmentation warhead, and stood up in full view of the approaching aircraft.

As the Pucara flew low, already firing its guns and creating lines of spitting soil that raced dangerously towards Andrew, he coolly fitted the Stinger's shoulder-rest into his shoulder, held the foregrip, squinted into the aiming sight and pressed the trigger located in the grip.

Armed with an infrared seeker and sensors that could track its target by the heat of its exhausts, the Stinger's surface-to-air missile streaked upwards and hit the Pucara as it was levelling out to ascend. The plane exploded with a mighty roar, turning into a spectacular ball of searing white flame and boiling black smoke, with its debris thrown far and wide, to rain down on the field. Andrew lowered the Stinger to his side and raised his free hand in the air, clenching his fist.

'How's that, fucker?' he bawled.

'I don't think he's going to answer,' Ricketts said. 'I think the cat's got his tongue.'

Andrew laughed and shook his head, as if bemused by Ricketts's statement, then hugged the Stinger to his chest. 'Sheer poetry,' he said.

Parkinson watched the ball of fire shrinking away in the sky, disappearing in the smoke being dispersed by the wind. 'I think the closer we get to Port Stanley, the more exposed we'll become. We're going to have to restrict ourselves to night marches and hide out in the daylight. I think a long-term OP should be made right here. Get to it, gentlemen.'

A rectangular OP was constructed in no time and the men, hidden under its camouflaged roof, became one with the barren earth.

15

During the next ten days Parkinson and his men holed up in their OP and only ventured out on deep-penetration patrols or to ambush Argentinians on the snow-covered hills. Their unfortunate victims, mostly inexperienced conscripts, usually on foot patrol, invariably in small groups, were cut down with relative ease by a combination of Andrew's GPMG, the M16s of the other men and the occasional fragmentation grenade.

More than once, usually at night, Danny was called upon to despatch a guard, which he always did with his customary deadly skill. This was often the prelude to an attack on an enemy OP or radio station; once the attack was completed, the radio would be destroyed and the printed data removed by Major Parkinson, to be relayed from the SAS OP to HQ on the *Hermes*, still out at sea with the fleet.

In their own small, anonymous way, Parkinson's group – and the many other SAS groups spread out across East Falkland – caused confusion and fear among the enemy, while also disrupting their communications and practising psychological warfare, or 'psyops' against them, so making the advance on Port Stanley easier for the other British troops.

When not thus engaged, the men hid out in their damp, claustrophobic, camouflaged OP, either observing and detailing enemy troop and aircraft movements or listening to the progress of the war on the BBC World Service. Through the latter they learnt that although the British now had air superiority, a briefly revitalized Argentinian Air Force was relentlessly bombing British forces on Fitzroy, Bluff Cove and Mount Kent.

'That won't last too long,' Gumboot said with an air of satisfaction. 'If they're the same as the Argies we encountered at Darwin and Goose Green – the ones who didn't have the nerve to climb out of their bleedin' trenches – I'd say those pilots will soon be finding excuses to have themselves grounded.'

'The Argentinians on Pebble Island were courageous,' Ricketts said, 'and if their pilots are of the same calibre, they could fight on for ever.'

'No way,' Gumboot replied. 'We've demolished half of their fucking planes. They're now flying on a wing and a prayer, just waiting to come down.'

'Meanwhile they're doing a lot of damage,' Andrew said, carefully oiling his weapons, 'so it's not over yet.'

More encouraging was the news that the British were patrolling the mountains around Port Stanley. When, on 11 June, Parkinson learnt from HQ that the battle for Port Stanley was about to begin, with night attacks against the major mountains of East Falkland – Longdon, Two Sisters and Harriet – he decided it was time to move on.

'We've done all we can do here,' he informed the men lying, half frozen, on both sides of him in their dug-outs in the OP. 'There's no more need for reconnaissance or harassment in this area. It's time to be heading for Port Stanley, where we'll be of more use.'

'When do we go?' Ricketts asked him.

'Why not right now?' Parkinson replied rhetorically, having already made up his mind. 'Let's pack up our kit, fill in the OP and get moving. We can march throughout the night while the main attacks are being launched, arriving at Port Stanley some time tomorrow. That's when we'll be useful.'

The men did as they were told, dismantling the OP, filling in the dug-out and carefully hiding anything that would reveal they had been there. Then they set off on the road to Port Stanley.

Marching throughout the night, sticking close to the coastline, intending to come in south of Port Stanley, they were whipped constantly by heavy wind, sleet and snow. They were, however, encouraged by the sounds and sights of battle, most a couple of miles to the north where the attacks on Mount Harriet, Tumbledown and Mount William were being undertaken by Nos 4 and 7 Infantry Regiments, as well as the crack 5 Marine Battalion.

The battle being engaged, the night sky was criss-crossed with dazzling white phosphorus tracers, coloured crimson, yellow and blue by fire, stained black by smoke. For most of the march they could hear 155mm and 105mm Argentinian artillery, the return fire of the 4.5in guns of the fleet, 105mm howitzers, 66mm anti-tank rockets, exploding 81mm mortar shells, chattering machine-guns and whining, growling aircraft, most of them British. Other explosions, Parkinson assumed, were being caused by enemy minefields, which reminded him to warn the patrol to watch the ground in front of them, as best they could, in the stormy, snow-whitened darkness.

When dawn broke they found themselves in a rugged, hilly, mist-wreathed landscape devastated by war. The battle for the three mountains around Port Stanley had been fought with bullets, grenades and bayonets under cover of mortar, artillery and machine-gun fire. Now, in an area pock-marked with shell holes, some caused by mines, the enemy trenches and sangars camouflaged in rocky outcrops were scorched black and filled with corpses buried in debris.

Luckier, but not looking appreciative, were the hundreds of weary, shocked Argentinian prisoners who were being marched at gunpoint to makeshift camps of barbed wire and canvas, where they would be held until the reconquest of Port Stanley, then almost certainly shipped back to Argentina.

Making their way across the rocky ridges and rugged spines of the hills around Port Stanley, Parkinson and his group came into contact with battle-weary Scots Guardsmen, Welsh Guards, Marines, Commandos, Paratroopers, Gurkhas, REMFs, and even Forward Observers from 148 Commando Battery Royal Artillery.

Port Stanley was now visible from the heights, though covered in smoke from the exploding shells of the Naval gunline bombarding the airport, the racecourse and Sapper Hill. As the port had not yet been taken, British and Argentinian aircraft were still flying to and fro, the former bombing Port Stanley and inland, the latter attacking the Fleet. Helicopters, all British, were landing and taking off in a race to transport the growing numbers of wounded to the Forward Dressing Stations of Teal and Fitzroy, or the Main Dressing Station at Ajax, further away on San Carlos Water.

All of this could be seen from the desolate, mountainous region, south of Port Stanley, through which Parkinson and his men were resolutely marching. They were therefore surprised when they saw another farmhouse, isolated at the end of a track that snaked between windswept fields, being used by Argentinian troops. As the house offered a clear view of Port Stanley, it was clearly an observation post.

Parkinson signalled his men to go belly-down,

then he studied the house through binoculars.

'No doubt about it,' he told Ricketts. 'It's being used as an OP. There's a temporary aerial on the roof and a telescope thrusting out of one window. They're observing the movements of our troops around Port Stanley. Passing the info to their aircraft and big guns. We must have wandered into one of the few areas still not held by our own men. This is an Argie stronghold.'

Ricketts glanced about him, at the bleak, rolling hills, seeing nothing but swirling snow, wind-blown gorse, and the boats of the British Fleet, some bombed, still smouldering and sinking, in the grey sea beyond. 'The only Argies I see are outside that house,' he told Major Parkinson.

'Which means there are more *inside* the house.'

'So I suggest we take out the house and then be on our way – in fact all the way down to Port Stanley, to meet the rest of the Regiment. What say you, boss?'

'I say we don't have a choice, Sergeant. We go around it or through it.'

'Let's go through it, boss.'

Doubtless because this OP was close to Port

Stanley and surrounded by an advancing British army, instead of a single sentry distractedly studying his own feet, it was guarded by a pair of three-man trenches, one on each side of the dirt track leading up to its gardens. Both slit trenches had machine-gun emplacements, which made them formidable.

'A short, sharp shock,' Parkinson whispered.

'Fragmentation grenades to clear the trenches,' Ricketts suggested, 'then smoke grenades to cover our run up to the house. That should just about do it.'

'Let's hope so,' Parkinson said.

Signalling with his hands, he sent Danny and Andrew in opposite directions, both crouched low and advancing on either side of the dirt track, offered slight protection by the fall of the land in the frost-covered fields. As they were doing this, Parkinson, Ricketts and Gumboot, still flat on their bellies, covered the house with their M16s and SLRs. Danny and Andrew then also dropped down, both in protective furrows, and crawled forward, each on opposite sides of the dirt track, until they were in line with the slit trenches, just behind the line of vision of the sentries. They were out of sight for a moment, as if they had never existed, though some snow was then seen to move where they were obviously contorting to get at their webbing. Then two hands appeared, one on each side of the trenches, swinging in deceptive slow motion, releasing the smoke grenades.

One of the sentries glanced sideways, hearing the noise of Danny's throw, and shouted a warning – too late – as the smoke grenade fell into the trench. Danny's grenade exploded noisily, followed immediately by Andrew's, then the fragmentation grenades also looped into the trenches, even as smoke was billowing up to choke the panicking sentries. The second explosions were catastrophic, devastating the trenches, with soil and debris spewed at the sky on billowing mushrooms of black smoke.

The screaming of the sentries caught in the explosions was drowned out by the sudden, savage roar of the SAS small arms.

'Go!' Parkinson bellowed, jumping up and running forward, followed closely by Ricketts and Gumboot as Danny and Andrew, also jumping to their feet, ran in towards one another to check the trenches. Ignoring the trenches, Parkinson, Ricketts and Gumboot raced straight for the house, firing from the hip, hidden by the smoke from the grenades and further protected by the element of surprise. As they plunged into the smokescreen created by the grenades, Danny and Andrew were closing in on both sides of them, converging on the trenches, and putting paid to the survivors, if such there were, by automatically peppering them with deadly bursts from their SLRs.

Oblivious, Parkinson, Ricketts and Gumboot were bursting out of the clouds of smoke, still firing from the hip, to race over the gardens in front of the house where the enemy troops were bellowing, screaming, quivering like bowstrings, and collapsing in the hail of bullets from the three semi-automatic weapons.

Reaching the front of the house, where trucks and a jeep where parked, Parkinson quickly scanned the area, noted the dead and dying – no threat posed here any more – then pressed his spine to the wall beside the front door, which was open. A savage burst of gunfire suddenly came from the windows as Ricketts and Gumboot, ducking low and diving forward, reached the other side of the door, from where the latter hurled a grenade into the house.

The subsequent explosion filled the house with flame and smoke, letting Parkinson slip in through the front door, already firing his weapon in a wide arc taking in the whole room. He saw vague figures in smoke and dust, rising up, falling down, then Ricketts and Gumboot were right there behind him, also firing their weapons. The room reverberated with screaming, but no shots were fired back. Parkinson went in further, shooting anything that moved, and only stopped when the smoke escaped through the open door and smashed windows, letting him see that the house was devastated – and that all the Argentinians on the floor were either dead or dying.

'There's their damned radio,' Ricketts said. 'Fuck that for a joke.' He let rip with a burst of fire from his M16. The radio, which had been receiving British broadcasts, exploded and burst into flames. '*Adiós*,' Ricketts said.

Parkinson was already rifling through the Army documents littering the kitchen table, which had been used for a desk, when a mortar shell exploded in the front garden, shaking the whole house, spewing dust and soil through the smashed windows.

'Christ!' Parkinson exclaimed softly, not even ducking, but looking out through the front door, 'was that us or them?'

Before Ricketts could answer, Danny raced

through the open front door, practically pirouetting to a halt, to gasp: 'We're surrounded by Argies! They were dug in all around the house, as far as four or five hundred yards out. They're moving in on us, Major.'

'*All* around us?' Parkinson asked as Andrew followed Danny into the house.

'Yes, boss!' Andrew said, his eyes as bright as diamonds. 'We're completely surrounded, boss.'

'Damn!' Parkinson hammered his fist on the table, glanced at the door and windows, then focused his gaze on the charred, bloody, dead men in the room. 'They're not about to take prisoners after this. They won't have time for small talk.'

'We have to leave,' Ricketts said. 'It's get out or be done in.'

'Two-man teams,' Parkinson said. 'One man looking after the other. Out the back door and run like the clappers, trusting in God or luck. You and Danny go first, Ricketts, then Andrew and Gumboot.'

'What about you, boss?'

'Two-man teams,' Parkinson said. 'Each man depending on the other. It's the best – the only – way in these circumstances. Get going, Ricketts.'

'That leaves you alone, boss.'

'Two and two, Ricketts. *Go!*'

'You're the CO of the Squadron,' Ricketts said, 'so I can't leave you here.'

'I'm responsible for my men,' Parkinson said, 'and they have to take orders.' Another mortar shell exploded out in the front garden, shaking the house, showering more soil and dust through the open door and smashed windows. When the explosion had done its worst and subsided, the hoarse shouts and firing weapons of the Argentinians could more clearly be heard. 'Time's up,' Parkinson continued. 'And an order is an order, Sergeant Ricketts, so get the hell out of here.' He turned to Andrew. 'Leave the GPMG, Trooper Winston. Goodbye and good luck.'

Andrew unshouldered the heavy GPMG, laid it carefully on the floor, then stood up and took a deep breath. 'OK,' he said, 'who goes first?'

'You and Gumboot,' Ricketts said. 'And don't waste any time.'

'Yeah, boss,' Andrew said.

'I'm staying behind,' Gumboot said to Parkinson, 'and that's all there is to it. This Squadron needs its damned CO. With your permission, boss, I'm saying get the hell out the door with that handsome black bastard.'

Parkinson glanced at Ricketts, who nodded his approval. 'As you wish, Gumboot,' Parkinson said, sounding a little choked up. 'Good luck to you.'

'Good luck, boss.'

Holding his M16 in the Belfast cradle, Andrew marched through the shattered front room, kicking furniture aside, letting it fall over the dead men, and didn't stop until he reached the back door. Leaning sideways, he glanced out of the window, saw nothing immediately threatening, so checked that Parkinson was behind him, then took a deep breath. He grabbed the door handle, jerked the door open, screamed 'Go!' and hurled himself out.

Parkinson followed – and was followed almost immediately by Ricketts and Danny – just as a mortar shell exploded in the back yard, spewing fire and smoke, tearing up more soil and debris. The four men, breaking into two groups, raced hell for leather across the broad field, aware only of the roaring, erupting earth and the need to be free of it.

Back in the house, Gumboot mounted the machine-gun on its tripod, loaded a 200-round magazine, and sat patiently in that room filled with dead, waiting for the enemy. Their gun barrels appeared first, poking in through both smashed windows, and Gumboot pressed the trigger of the machine-gun even as the Argentinians' gun barrels spat flame in his general direction, then blindly raked the room.

The machine-gun shook his body, pierced his flesh with countless spikes, then he realized that the shaking and the burning were part of his dying.

The hail of billets threw him backwards, made him gasp, killed all feeling, but he had a sudden glimpse of his wife at home in Devon, tending the garden, not particularly attractive and inclined to wander at times, but the only woman he'd ever cared about or felt the pain of love for.

She wasn't bad at all, he thought as he died, *and life could have been* . . .

He was dead before the men who had shot him burst into the room.

16

Ricketts and Danny zigzagged through the eruptions of mortar shells, glimpsing shadowy figures aiming at them through swirling smoke. Hearing gunshots, seeing the soil spitting around them, firing back as they ran, crouched low, they somehow managed to get away.

Escaping from the chaos, stumbling down a rocky, frost-covered gradient, Ricketts, followed by Danny, came to a halt in a gully filled with snow, offering a panoramic view of Port Stanley and the war being waged there.

Parkinson and Andrew were there, also, the trooper already on the radio, calling in grid references to the fleet and asking for aircraft support. The Sea Harriers were there in minutes, bombing the hell out of the hilltop, turning it into an inferno of flame and smoke before giving the all-clear.

'Damn it,' Parkinson said. 'We can't leave him there. He's got to be taken all the way. Who's going back with me?'

'We're *all* going,' Ricketts said.

They clambered back up the hill and returned to a field of dead, the ground surrounding the house pock-marked by shell holes and littered with scorched, tattered bodies. The farmhouse, as Andrew had instructed, had been left intact.

'I hate giving credit to the RAF,' Andrew said; looking in admiration at the dreadful carnage around the untouched farmhouse, 'but in this case I have to. The proof's in the pudding, right?'

Hardened though they were, they had a problem with Gumboot. He had been shot so many times, by so many, he looked no more than a heap of tattered, dust-covered rags, buried in overturned, splintered furniture. Choking back their rage and grief, they dragged him out from where he lay, rolled him onto a makeshift stretcher of wood and Argentinian webbing, then proceeded to carry him down to Port Stanley.

Ricketts was silent, but his cheeks were stained with tears.

'Oh, Lord, my man,' Andrew said, 'but this is one death we don't need.'

Baby-faced Danny revealed little: out ahead, on point, leading them downhill, he never relaxed his guard for a moment, keeping his thoughts to himself.

Major Parkinson was more emotional, having to fight to control himself; he managed to do so by taking the radio from Andrew, getting in touch with HQ, and filling them in on events.

'Just part of the damned job,' Andrew was heard to mutter as they entered liberated Port Stanley. 'We all pay our dues and take our chances, so no point thinking about it.'

'One more fucking word,' Ricketts said, 'and I'll tear your head off. Do you understand, Andrew?'

'Yes, boss,' Andrew said.

Ricketts smiled and placed his hand on Andrew's shoulder, squeezing gently, affectionately. 'Sorry, Trooper.'

'No sweat, boss.'

Still carrying Gumboot on his improvised stretcher, they marched through the recaptured streets of Port Stanley, past wooden-framed houses miraculously untouched, damaged British ships still smouldering in the docks, 42 Commando Marines, the Red Berets of 2 Para, and dejected Argentinian prisoners huddled around open fires beside piles of discarded weapons and helmets. They also marched past traffic jams of Land Rovers, troop trucks, Panhard armoured cars and Mercedes jeeps; under a sky filled with Sea King, Lynx, Scout, Chinook and Wessex helicopters, as well as Sea Harriers and Vulcan bombers – marched resolutely to the one place where they knew that Gumboot, even dead, would wish to be on this great day of liberation.

Resting the stretcher that bore the body of their beloved friend on a couple of tables in the Upland Goose bar, Ricketts and his troopers, trying desperately not to cry, ordered drinks for everyone in the house.

They were not refused service.

17

In Port Stanley, at 9.00pm local time on 14 June, 1982, Major General Mario Menéndez formally surrendered all the Argentinian Armed Forces in East and West Falkland to Major-General J.J. Moore. The British flag was raised again over Government House.

Throughout the next couple of days, while thousands of dejected Argentinian soldiers were rounded up by British forces and imprisoned near Stanley airport, before being shipped back to Argentina, the members of the various five-man SAS teams came marching into Port Stanley to be reunited with their friends, swap stories, and express their grief over the death of Gumboot, whose body had already been shipped back to Hereford.

During lively drinking sessions in the Upland Goose, when Ricketts, Danny, Andrew and

Major Parkinson were trading experiences with their friends, it emerged that Captain Grenville had linked up with other SBS men, returned to the fleet, then taken part in the daring SBS raid designed to set fire to oil storage tanks in Stanley's harbour installations, coming ashore from high-speed raiding craft and withdrawing without serious casualties. Also in the harbour at that time were Captain Hailsham, Corporal Paddy Clarke and Trooper Taff Burgess, who had actually managed to infiltrate enemy defences to hide in the hulk of a wrecked boat, keep a watch on the harbour, and report back to the fleet with daily details of Argentinian movements. Other groups had, like Parkinson and his men, simply foraged across the land, disrupting enemy communications, harassing their patrols and committing many invaluable acts of sabotage. SAS casualties, with the tragic exception of Trooper Gillis, had been minimal.

'So here's to Gumboot,' Ricketts said.

They all touched glasses, saluting their dead friend, then drank to his memory.

A few days after the surrender of the Argentinian forces, when the harbour was secured and the cleaning-up process had begun, the media descended like wolves on Port Stanley,

anxious to tell the 'true' story of the Battle for the
Falklands.

Though the fighting had stopped, explosions
were still taking place in the hills around Port
Stanley as anti-personnel mines were located and
set off by British sappers. Piles of abandoned
weapons, equipment and other stores were being
removed. On the runway of Stanley airport,
damaged Pucaras were surrounded by strewn
debris, stores, ammunition, flapping tents and
the burnt-out skeletons of other vehicles. The
walls of the terminal were scarred with bullet
holes, when not completely destroyed by the
explosions of shells from the fleet's big guns.
The wind that howled and blew sleet through
the broken windows of the same building, also
froze the thousands of dejected, mud-covered
Argentinian prisoners who were huddled near
the airstrip, wrapped in blankets and ponchos,
waiting to be embarked on the *Canberra* and
shipped home. In Port Stanley itself there was an
acute water shortage because, though the wooden
buildings remained untouched, the town's sole
filtration plant had been destroyed in the
bombings.

As they investigated the area, interviewing victorious British troops and defeated Argentinians,

the reporters gradually picked up a lot of seemingly fantastic stories about the SAS. Intrigued, they tried to track down some members of the legendary Regiment and ended up, perhaps inevitably, in the Upland Goose.

They could find no members of the SAS. The Squadron had packed up and gone, leaving no trace behind.

'The SAS?' a local said to one of the journalists. 'That regiment's just a myth, mate. You guys must have invented it.'

That remark would have been hugely appreciated in the pubs of Hereford.